BOYS'
&
SEARCH AND

Howard Korder

Methuen Drama

Methuen Drama **Modern Plays**

Boys' Life copyright © 1988 by Howard Korder
Search and Destroy copyright © 1990, 1992 by Howard Korder
The right of Howard Korder to be identified as the author of this
work has been asserted by him in accordance with the Copyright, Designs
and Patents Act, 1988

This volume first published in Great Britain in 1997 by Methuen Drama

A CIP catalogue record for this book is available from the British Library

Papers used by Methuen Drama are natural, recyclable
products made from wood grown in sustainable forests.
The manufacturing processes conform to the environmental regulations of
the country of origin.

ISBN 0 413 71200 1

Typeset by Deltatype Ltd, Birkenhead, Merseyside

Contents

BOYS' LIFE

for Lois

Boys' Life was first presented by Lincoln Center Theater (Andre Bishop, Artistic Director; Bernard Gersten, Executive Producer) at the Mitzi E. Newhouse Theater in New York City on 29 February 1988. The Atlantic Theater Company was as follows:

Don	Jordan Lage
Phil	Steven Goldstein
Jack	Clark Gregg
Karen	Mary McCann
Man	Todd Weeks
Maggie	Felicity Huffman
Lisa	Melissa Bruder
Girl	Robin Spielberg
Carla	Théo Cohan

Directed by W. H. Macy
Designed by James Wolk
Costumes by Donna Zakowska
Lighting by Steve Lawnick
Sound by Aural Fixation
Original Music by David Yazbek

Boys' Life was originally produced by Lincoln Center Theater, New York City.

Characters

Jack
Don
Phil
Man
Lisa
Maggie
Karen
Girl
Carla
All in their late twenties

Time
The present.
Various intervals over the course of a year.

Place
A large city.

Scene One

Don's *bedroom.* **Jack** *smoking a joint.* **Phil** *lying on the floor, wearing a set of headphones.* **Don** *sitting in his underwear. Bottles, clothes, books scattered on the floor. One a.m.*

Jack   Remember the nineteen-seventies?

Don   Sure. Sort of.

Jack   Name three things that happened in the nineteen-seventies.

Don   This is like a trick question, right?

Jack   I'll give you one minute.

Phil *(loudly, tapping phones)*   I haven't heard this since college, you know?

Jack *(smiling and nodding)*   Eat me, Phil.

Phil *(not hearing)*   Okay!

Jack   Give up?

Don   That wasn't a minute.

Jack   Let's go.

Phil   *Great* bass line.

Don   Um . . .

Jack   Do it!

Don   Um . . . Watergate? And . . . uh . . . *(Pause.)* The Sex Pistols . . . and uh . . . *(Pause.)* Did I say Watergate?

Jack   I rest my case.

Don   Ah . . . giant leap for a man?

Jack   Oh, hang it *up*, Don.

Don   Did I *say* Watergate?

Jack   You're losing it, Don. Your mind is going.

Don   The nineteen-seventies.

Jack   You're rotting on the vine.

Phil (*imitating an electric guitar*)   War-raaang! (*Pause.*)

Jack   Well, *I'm* having fun.

Don   Me too.

Jack   I know you are. We live in thrilling days, Don.

Don   We *do*.

Jack   And I think that's swell.

Don   I do too.

Jack   I know you do. You're an agreeable guy. And I've been meaning to tell you this, really, if someone came up to me and asked, 'Now this *Don* fellow, what's he all about?' I'd have to tell him, well, darn it, Don, Don's an *agreeable* guy.

Don   I'd go along with that.

Jack   Would you go along with a toast?

Don (*picking up a beer*)   By all means.

Jack   To you, Don, for being the post-modern kind of nut you are.

Don   Thanks, Jack.

Jack   To Phil, a great guy in spite of some desperate handicaps.

Phil (*not hearing*)   Okay!

Jack   And to me, for being perfect.

Don   Not easy.

Jack   And Don, to our times together. From campus cut-ups to wasted potentials.

Don   It feels like years.

Jack   It *has* been years.

Don   We are getting old.

Jack   To our parents, Don. To the dream they called America. To the Big Kidder upstairs. To, ah . . .

Phil (*imitating drums*)   Da-dum-dum-dum-dum-*dum* . . .

Don   The ladies!

Jack   Don, a toast, a very *special* toast, to the ladies.

Don   Oh my.

Jack   Yes indeed. Where would we be without them?

Don   We'd be nowhere.

Jack   We wouldn't be *here*.

Don   We wouldn't even *exist*.

Jack   We would not.

Don   It's a sobering thought.

Jack   It's food for thought.

Don   It's a thought to think. (*Pause.*)

Jack   Well, no sense in blaming them for it now.

Don   It's a dead issue.

Jack   It's all said and done. 'Cause when you come right down to it . . .

Phil   I *love* this part . . .

Jack   A man . . .

Don   Is a *man*.

Jack   He *is* a man.

Don   By *any* other name.

Jack   He'd still smell.

Don   Amen.

Jack   God*damn*.

Don   Goddamn *shit*.

Jack   *Cocksucking* shit.

Don   Goddamn shit-eating asshole *scumbags!* (**Jack** *breaks out into a wolf howl.* **Don** *joins in. Pause.*) You know, you'd never have this kind of talk with a woman.

Jack   No, you wouldn't. And I want you always to remember this, Don. When you're old and pissing in your day-bed, remember who brought you out of the jungle and shaved off your fur.

Don (*in a zombie-like monotone*)   It was you master. You teach Don to walk like man.

Jack   And you *better* be grateful. (*He drags on the joint.*) Here. Finish that off. Come on, come on. (*He passes the joint to* **Don**. **Don** *takes a hit. Silence. He smiles.*) What are you smiling about?

Don   Nah, I was just thinking.

Jack   Uh-huh.

Don   I used to really want to be an astronaut, you know? Be up there. The quiet. Walter Cronkite talking about me to millions of people. But I wouldn't have to *listen*.

Jack   So?

Don   So I'd still like to be an astronaut.

Jack   Maybe you will be, Don. But even if you were . . . you'd still have to get out of bed in the morning.

Don (*thinking it over*)   Yeah. (*Pause.* **Phil** *takes off the headphones.*)

Phil   Emerson, Lake, and Palmer, man, whatever happened to them?

Jack   They all died horribly, Phil, in a bus crash.

Phil   They did? That's really depressing.

Jack   I thought it might be. (*Pause.*) Well, gentlemen. Anybody have a good fuck lately?

Phil   Does masturbation count? (*Blackout.*)

Scene Two

A child's bedroom. **Phil** *and* **Karen** *standing at opposite ends of the room, facing each other. The bed is piled with coats. Sounds of a party filter in from outside.*

Phil   Well, there *you* are.

Karen   Yes.

Phil   And here I am.

Karen   Yes.

Phil   So here we are, both of us. Together.

Karen   Talking.

Phil   Right here in the same room.

Karen   It's pretty amazing. (*Pause.*) Enjoying the party?

Phil   Oh yes. Certainly. Yes yes yes.

Karen   Mmmm.

Phil   No.

Karen   Oh.

Phil   Not in the larger sense.

Karen   Why did you come?

Phil   I was invited. I mean . . . Jack invited me.

Karen   And you do everything Jack says.

Phil   No, I . . . he's my friend. My oldest friend. (*Pause.*) You look great tonight, Karen.

Karen   Thanks.

Phil   No, I mean it. Just wonderful. (*Pause.*)

Karen   You look good.

Phil   No.

Karen   You do.

Phil   No I don't.

Karen   Really, you do.

Phil   Do I?

Karen   What do you want, Phil?

Phil   Well, I don't *want* anything. I just wanted to . . . say hello.

Karen   Hello.

Phil   Yes, well. (*Pause.*) That's lovely, what you have on, what is it?

Karen   A dress.

Phil   I've always admired your sense of humour, Karen.

Karen   What do you want, Phil? (*The door opens and a* **Man** *pops his head in.*)

Man   Oh. I'm sorry.

Karen   We're almost done.

Man   Oh. Well. Fine. I'll, ah . . . fine. (*He exits, closing the door.*)

Phil   What was that all about?

Karen   What?

Phil   That. That guy.

Karen   I don't know.

Phil   Well you seemed pretty familiar with him.

Karen   Are you feeling okay?

Phil   Hmm? Oh, sure. Things are going really really great for me right now. Just fine. I have my own partition now, over at the office, they put up one of those, ah . . . so *that's* really good. And I'm going to the spa a lot, I'm working

ou – well, I can't use the machines 'cause you know of my
back, but I love the Jacuzzi, so, actually, it's strange, 'cause
I fell asleep in it, in the whirlpool, and when I woke up I
had this incredible headache, I mean it would *not* go away,
I felt this thing here like the size of a peach pit, I went for
a *blood* test, I was convinced I, you hear all this stuff now,
the way it's spreading, I mean I'm not – but I was sure I
had it.

Karen   Had what?

Phil   It. You know. (*Pause.*)

Karen   And?

Phil   I didn't. So. (*Pause.* **Karen** *looks at the door.*) Anyway,
it's funny we both happened to turn up here tonight, isn't
it, 'cause I was just thinking, I was wondering . . . I mean,
it's a couple of months since I last spoke to you and I was
just *wondering* if we were still, you know, seeing each other.

Karen   *Seeing* each other.

Phil   Yes.

Karen   No. (*Pause.*)

Phil   All right.

Karen   We were never seeing each other, Phil.

Phil   Well, no, not actually *seeing* . . .

Karen   We slept together once.

Phil   Twice.

Karen   You left before I woke up.

Phil   Okay. Yeah, but . . . I mean, *everybody* does that.

Karen   And you never called.

Phil   Now . . . now about *that*, you see, I was involved in
a very bad kind of situation then, and I wasn't really in a
position to, ah . . . as much as I *wanted* to . . . and I *did*,
very, very –

Karen What do you want?

Phil (*pause*) Well, I'd like another shot at it.

Karen At what?

Phil At you. To get to know you.

Karen I'm really not worth the effort, Phil.

Phil You're seeing someone else, right?

Karen That's got nothing to –

Phil You *are* seeing someone.

Karen Not actually *seeing* . . .

Phil No, no, it's fine. Early bird and all that stuff. I'm fine. Everything is fine.

Karen It's got nothing to do with you, Phil. There's just a lot of things I have to work through right now. But I like you, I do. You're . . . you're a wonderful person.

Phil You're a wonderful person too, Karen.

Karen Well, so are you, Phil.

Phil That's right. We both are. (*He hugs* **Karen**.) Listen to this. A guy in my office has a cabin upstate. He never uses it. It's on the edge of a beautiful freshwater lake. Why don't we go there, just the two of us, we spend the weekend, relax, get out of the city . . . do some straight thinking. What do you say?

Karen No.

Phil Is it because of this guy you're seeing?

Karen Well, I'm not actually *seeing* –

Phil Then what is it?

Karen It's just not a good idea.

Phil It's not?

Karen No. Not at all. (*Pause.*) You're touching my

breasts, Phil. (*The **Man** pops his head through the door.*)

Man Oh gosh. Beg pardon. (*He shuts the door.*)

Phil I think about you a lot, Karen.

Karen You do.

Phil Yes. At work, you know, the laundromat, in the shower . . . places like that. (*Pause.*) I mean that in the positive sense.

Karen I'm not worth the trouble.

Phil It's just two days out of your life, Karen. This could turn out to be something really special, it'll be over before you know it.

Karen You're making this very difficult.

Phil I'm making it incredibly *easy*. Come up to the country with me.

Karen Phil –

Phil Come.

Karen Please, Phil –

Phil I'm asking for a *chance*.

Karen Oh, no. Oh no. This is coming at a very bad time for me. I don't think I can handle this right now. My life is a real big mess, okay, and . . . I read that by the time you're five you've already developed the major patterns for the rest of your life. I mean whether you're going to be basically happy or . . . a fireman, a lesbian, whatever. And of course it's not fair at all, because nobody tells a little kid anything about that. But that's the way it is. So I've been thinking about this. And it occurs to me that somewhere along the line I screwed up really bad. I made a very poor choice about something and now there's nothing I can do to change it.

Phil I think I love you.

Karen You haven't been listening.

Phil   Of course I have. You were talking about your childhood, right? I love you.

Karen   No, Phil. I'm really very flattered –

Phil   I'm not saying it to flatter you, Karen. We're not talking about your drapes. We're talking about this very real and undeniable feeling I have for you. So you're not happy. I think I can sense that from what you just told me. But *nobody's* happy. That's the way things are *supposed* to be. You think I'm happy? I'm not happy, I'm miserable.

Karen   I am too.

Phil   I know you are. That's why I feel so close to you. Karen? I can *make* you happy. And you can make me happy. We can help each other.

Karen   You just said that nobody is happy.

Phil   I didn't *mean* that. I feel so crazy when I'm with you I don't know what I'm saying. I love you.

Karen   No – please –

Phil   I love you. I'm sick with needing you. It's an actual disease. I'm all swollen and rotten inside, my brain is decomposing, and it's because of you.

Karen   What's wrong with you, Phil?

Phil   I'm dying without you, Karen. I'm serious. Has anyone ever told you anything like that? Ever?

Karen   No. Never.

Phil   Because no one has ever loved you as much as I do. Jesus, Karen, help me! (*The* **Man** *pops his head through the door.*)

Man   Excuse me . . .

Phil   What? What do you want?

Man   Well . . . my coat . . .

Phil   In a minute.

Man   I've been waiting –

Phil   GO AWAY! (*The* **Man** *shuts the door.*) I love you.

Karen   For how long?

Phil   Until I'm in my grave. Longer. For ever.

Karen   No, I mean . . . how long would we have to be away for?

Phil   As long as you want. We don't even have to come back.

Karen   I was thinking just the weekend.

Phil   Yes, yes, the weekend. A day. An hour. A single second.

Karen   I have pasta class Monday nights.

Phil   Great. Fabulous. (*Pause.*)

Karen   I wish I could, Phil. It's not that I don't want to . . .

Phil   If you want to, just say yes. Don't worry about the rest.

Karen   I can't.

Phil   Then just say maybe.

Karen   If I say maybe, you'll think I'm saying yes.

Phil   I won't. I promise. I'm very clear on maybe. (*Pause.*) Please, Karen. Give me a crumb. Throw me a line.

Karen   Oh, let me think about it, I have to . . . okay. Maybe. I'd like to – I don't know, maybe.

Phil   Maybe. Maybe. Thank you, Karen. You won't be sorry. I'm crazy about you. You know that, don't you?

Karen   I'm not worth it, Phil. Really.

Phil   This is the happiest day of my life. (*He kisses her and eases her down onto the bed. He climbs on top of her and starts to caress her. The* **Man** *enters.*)

Man Look, I'm very sorry about this, but I need my coat. (**Karen** *breaks away and sits on the edge of the bed*.) Sorry.

Karen That's all right. We're done.

Man Are you?

Phil (*rising from the bed*) Come on. Let's get back to the party.

Karen No, you go ahead.

Phil You're not coming?

Karen In a minute.

Phil (*moving towards her*) Is everything okay?

Karen Yes, yes, it's really – Phil, no please, please, just stay away – (*To the* **Man**.) Look, I'm sorry, I – (*Turning away*.) Oh God I hate myself so *much*! (*She runs out of the room*.)

Phil (*following her*) Karen, wait a – (*She slams the door*.) Shit. Shit shit shit! (*He leans against the door. Silence*.)

Man Interesting girl, isn't she? In her way?

Phil Huh?

Man Personality-wise.

Phil How would you know?

Man She was sort of my date.

Phil Oh.

Man But I don't think it's gonna work out. High-strung, you know? I got better things to do. (*Pause*.)

Phil We're in love.

Man You and her?

Phil Yes.

Man Congratulations.

Phil Thanks. (*Pause*.)

Man   You want to reimburse me for cab fare or what?
(*Blackout.*)

Scene Three

Lights up on **Jack** *and* **Maggie** *sitting on a bench opposite a
playground in a city park.* **Jack** *smokes a joint.* **Maggie***, wheezing
heavily, wears a motley exercise suit with race number tied around her
chest below a small pin-on button. She has a pair of headphones in
her ears.*

Maggie   Oh God. Oh God.

Jack   Been doing some running, huh? (*Pause.* **Maggie** *pays
him no attention.*) Hey. (**Maggie** *turns to him.*) Out doing some
running, huh? (**Maggie** *taps her headphones, smiles curtly, and
turns away.*) *Excuse* me. (*He taps her shoulder.*)

Maggie   What?

Jack   I'm talking to you.

Maggie   Yes?

Jack   Asked you a question?

Maggie   What?

Jack   What's it *for*?

Maggie   Huh?

Jack   The race.

Maggie   We're jogging against apartheid.

Jack   Really.

Maggie   No. Of course not.

Jack   Oh. (*Pause.*) Interesting people, the Boers, you think?

Maggie   I wouldn't know. (*Pause.* **Maggie** *coughs violently.*)

Jack   Something wrong?

Maggie   I'm going to die.

Jack   You should catch your breath.

Maggie   What I'm trying to *do*.

Jack   (*noticing the button on her chest*)   May I? (*He leans in closely.*) Ah yes. 'Question Authority.'

Maggie   That's what it says.

Jack   I know – excuse me – that's a bad place for a button. It can restrict your circulation, should I take it off?

Maggie   Where'd you get that?

Jack   I beg your pardon, but I didn't 'get it' anywhere. It's something I have to know in my line of work.

Maggie   And what might that be?

Jack   I'm a cardiologist. (*Pause.*)

Maggie   Please go away.

Jack   Pardon?

Maggie   You heard me. I'm not in the mood for it. Go bother somebody else. (*Pause.* **Jack** *looks at her and turns away. Silence. Suddenly he leaps up.*)

Jack   (*out*)   HEY JASON! YO! *OFF* THE SWINGS! . . . YEAH, THAT'S RIGHT! (*Pause.*) I'LL COME OVER THERE! I'LL COME OVER THERE! YOU WANT ME TO COME O – (*Pause. He sits.*) Kid's looking for a brick in the head.

Maggie   Cute.

Jack   Yah.

Maggie   How old?

Jack   I dunno . . . five, six maybe.

Maggie   You don't know how old your kid is?

Jack   Hey. He's not *mine*.

Maggie   Sorry, it –

Jack   What do I look like? Come *on*.

Maggie   *Okay.*

Jack   I wouldn't have a kid like that. Give me some credit. (*Pause.*) He's my ward.

Maggie   Your ward.

Jack   Well, I'm more like his tutor.

Maggie   What do you teach him?

Jack   What do I *teach* him? I *teach* him about *life*. Don't play with matches . . . write down phone messages . . . that kind of thing. (*Pause.*) Ah, sorry I bothered you. I didn't mean to bother you.

Maggie   Yeah, well.

Jack   It's just you looked . . . in need.

Maggie   I'm not. (*Pause.*) What's ten k?

Jack   Pardon?

Maggie   Ten k, what is it?

Jack   Well, I think it comes to around six miles.

Maggie   Miles.

Jack   It's, you know, metric.

Maggie   Six *miles*? I'm gonna kill him.

Jack   Who?

Maggie   Nobody. A friend.

Jack   Must be quite a fella.

Maggie   He's an asshole. You know?

Jack   Sure. (*He offers her the joint.*) You want?

Maggie   No. Yes. (*She takes it.*) What am I doing? What am I doing?

Jack   Well, it looks to me like – JASON! OVER HERE!

WHAT ARE YOU, AN IDIOT? HOW MANY TIMES
AM I GONNA TELL YOU? STOP ACTING LIKE A
MONGOLOID AND GET OFF THE SWING! (*Pause.*)
WHAT? WHAT DID YOU SAY? (*Pause.*) THAT'S *RIGHT*
YOU SAID NOTHING! Let me tell you, that kid has a
mouth like a sewer. I don't know where he gets it from. *I'd*
have that kid horsewhipped. You can't do that though, can
you? They're delicate, aren't they? There are all kinds of
sociological factors involved. You smack them in the head,
next thing you know they're strolling through Arby's with a
high-powered rifle. And you're to blame.

Maggie   Come on.

Jack   You think I'm kidding? Nine out of ten experts will
agree with me. Have another hit.

Maggie   I shouldn't. (*She takes the joint. They look at each
other. Pause.*)

Jack   What's on the phones?

Maggie   Oh, nothing.

Jack   It's okay, I'm eclectic. Fred Waring Singers?

Maggie   No, it's nothing. Actual nothing. They're not
plugged in, see? (*Pause.*) You know how sometimes you just
can't stand to talk to someone? You know?

Jack   Your friend.

Maggie   It's not enough he's prancing around in spandex
pyjamas, he's got to keep telling me how *wonderful* it feels to
be *alive* on a day like this. And how he feels all this energy,
this *beautiful* energy *flowing* out of him. He's like a cheap
microwave.

Jack   Spandex pyjamas?

Maggie   It's his outfit. He's got all these . . . *outfits*, right?
He never just *wears* anything. (*Pause.*) Listen.

Jack   Yes.

Maggie   He gets his body waxed. I'm not kidding.

Jack Well.

Maggie Not a hair on him. He's from Portugal.

Jack Right.

Maggie So there you have it. (*Pause.*) Your kid's on the monkey bars, is that okay?

Jack He's not my kid.

Maggie Well, your whatever. Christ, I'm stoned. (*She giggles.*) You're not really a cardiologist.

Jack Not literally, no.

Maggie So are you trying to pick me up or what?

Jack I'm just sitting here.

Maggie You sit here often?

Jack I've got a lot of quality time on my hands. (*Pause.*) HEY! WHAT I SAY ABOUT HANGING UPSIDE DOWN, HUH? REMEMBER JUSTIN HENRY!

Maggie Who?

Jack That punk from *Kramer vs Kramer*. You know where he falls off the jungle gym? I made him watch it on the VCR. Now he wants to be in the movies, are you seriously involved?

Maggie Where?

Jack Your Portuguese friend.

Maggie Yeah, sure. We bought a sofa bed together. That counts for something, doesn't it, we both sleep on it. (*Pause.*) Ah, my God. He loves me, and I can't listen to him speak without looking for the carving knife. He's so . . . I mean, just what is going *on*? What are we *doing*? We drift into record shops, we wear nice clothes, we eat Cajun food, and what is all that? It's *garbage*, that's all it really is. Absolute . . . Where's the foundation, eh? Where's the . . . Look, I read the papers. He doesn't know it. The world is coming to an end. I'm not *kidding*. We need to be getting better, don't we? As a species? We should be improving. But we're not. The world is coming to an end and I'm spending my last moments thinking about . . . ach, who *knows*, sugar cones, skin cream, *nonsense*. Do you follow me?

Jack Yes. Yes, I –

Maggie I don't want to help other people. I say I do but I don't. I wish they would go away. Why doesn't that bother me? I don't know. I don't know. (*Pause.*)

Jack Great dope, huh?

Maggie Yeah. (*Silence.*)

Jack You ever see *It's a Wonderful Life*?

Maggie No.

Jack It's on TV all the time.

Maggie I haven't seen it. It's not a crime.

Jack Okay, Jimmy Stewart wants to kill himself, right? He's gonna jump off a bridge. Then this angel, bear with me, angel comes down, shows what the world would have been like if he'd never lived. And Jimmy Stewart realizes all the good he's done, without even knowing it.

Maggie Uh-huh.

Jack Didn't even *know* it.

Maggie So . . . what good have you done?

Jack Well, there you go. I might be another Mother Theresa, who can say?

Maggie Or you might just be selfish.

Jack Yeah, that's another possibility. (*Pause.*) I'm going to be finished here pretty soon.

Maggie How nice for you.

Jack Maybe we could get together.

Maggie How do you mean?

Jack   You know, get ... together. See what happens. I'm not trying to pick you up.

Maggie   What are you trying to do?

Jack   We could just talk (*Pause.*) Would you like to talk? I think we could talk about some things. (*Pause.*) Listen. I want to talk to you. (*Pause.*)

Maggie   What about your ward?

Jack   I'll drop him off.

Maggie   Where?

Jack   Where he *lives*.

Maggie   And where is that? (*Pause.*)

Jack   Well ... (*Pause.*) It would be interesting, wouldn't it?

Maggie   Yes. Very. But that's really not a *reason*. Besides ... you're married.

Jack   No I'm not.

Maggie   And you've got a kid.

Jack   No, I don't.

Maggie   And I think you're just kind of stoned and bored. (*Pause.*) Sorry. (*Silence.* **Jack** *stares out.*)

Jack   Look at that kid. I swear he's living with his head up his ass.

Maggie   Maybe he'll become a proctologist.

Jack   Yah.

Maggie   I'm Maggie.

Jack   Jack. Hello, Maggie.

Maggie   Hello, Jack.

Jack   Hi. (**Maggie** *starts out, turns back.*)

Maggie   Um ... (*She looks at him. Pause. She shakes her head and exits.* **Jack** *watches her go. Silence. He looks at his watch.*)

Jack ALL RIGHT, JASON, HAUL IT IN, TIME'S UP
... HEY, DID YOU HEAR ME? I SAID HAUL IT IN!
JASON, YOU GET OVER HERE PRONTO OR I'M
GONNA DECK YOU, UNDERSTAND? DADDY'S
GONNA BREAK YOUR LITTLE HEINIE! I'M GONNA
COUNT TO FIVE, JASON. ONE ... TWO ... THREE
... (*Pause.*) FOUR ... (*Pause.*) ALL RIGHT, THAT'S IT.
I'M CALLING MOMMY! (*Blackout.*)

Scene Four

Lights up. **Don** *and* **Lisa** *sitting at a table in a restaurant.*

Don Would you like another drink?

Lisa No. (*Pause.*) Do you understand what I mean?

Don . Uh-huh.

Lisa So why do they do it?

Don I don't know.

Lisa Like these men going around with all this, what,
military shit, you know, zippers everywhere, combat boots,
flak jackets, I mean people *died* in those things. And their
heads, they tilt their heads back, just a little, looking down
at you like, 'Hey, baby, you like this? I'm *dangerous*. Don't
fuck with me.' Who are they *kidding*? Those people, I mean
really dangerous people, they don't look like that. They laugh
at people like that. 'Hey baby.' Come on.

Don Sure.

Lisa And you see them in the stores, or they're getting
their *hair* cut, going, 'I want to look like so and so, you
know, like a rock star, or a *killer*.' Right? Like a *killer*. Why
is that? Why do they want to look like that?

Don You mean those guys?

Lisa Yes.

Don I don't know.

Lisa   Do they think it's attractive?

Don   I don't know.

Lisa   Am I supposed to fall to my knees?

Don   I don't know.

Lisa   Tell me, can't they see how *crude* they are?

Don   Probably not.

Lisa   Really? (*Pause.*)

Don   I don't know.

Lisa   Well, *I* don't know.

Don   You want another?

Lisa   No. Thanks. (*Pause.*)

Don   So what do you do when you're not waiting tables?

Lisa   How do you mean?

Don   I mean that's not all you do.

Lisa   Yes it is.

Don   Well, what do you *wanna* do . . .

Lisa   When I grow up?

Don   Yeah.

Lisa   I am grown up. This is as big as I get. (*Pause.*) I don't know, I'm taking some classes.

Don   You are.

Lisa   Over at the Art Students' League.

Don   Well.

Lisa   Sculpture.

Don   You must be really talented.

Lisa   Actually I'm not. (*Pause.*) Not talented enough.

Don   Maybe I could see your work.

Lisa   Maybe you could.

Don   I love sculpture.

Lisa   Huh.

Don   It's very rich, very sensuous. Humanistically speaking.

Lisa   Don.

Don   Yeah?

Lisa   Don't try so hard, okay? (*Pause.*)

Don   How about another drink?

Lisa   No.

Don   Come on.

Lisa   No, it's okay.

Don   *One* more . . .

Lisa   Are you trying to get me drunk?

Don   Of course.

Lisa   And then what happens?

Don   We go back to my place and I show you my flak jacket. (*Pause.*)

Lisa   I know that was supposed to be endearing.

Don   I was only making a joke.

Lisa   Who gave you the idea that was funny? (*Pause.*)

Don   I don't seem to be able to say the right thing to you.

Lisa   I'm sorry.

Don   I mean, you were talking before –

Lisa   I know. I'm . . . thanks for asking me out. I had a good time. Really.

Don If you think I'm trying to offend you –

Lisa Yes, yes, it's all right. Shall we go? (*Pause.* **Lisa** *reaches for the check.* **Don** *grabs it at the same time. They hold it between them.*) Please, Don, let me pay for this.

Don No, I've got it.

Lisa I'd like to. You paid for the film.

Don This is more.

Lisa Don't be silly.

Don It's covered.

Lisa Don, please.

Don I've got plenty of money, okay? You're my date, I'm paying for the fucking check! All right? (*Pause.*) I'm sorry, Lisa. I'm very sorry. You, ah . . . you . . . I can't figure you out.

Lisa I'm not that complicated.

Don We're not really hitting it off, are we?

Lisa We don't appear to be.

Don I do like sculpture.

Lisa Yes.

Don I don't know much about it. (*Pause.*) I don't know what I'm saying. (*Pause.*)

Lisa Do you enjoy being a man?

Don It's okay. (*Pause.*) Do you enjoy being a woman?

Lisa Not really. (*Pause.*)

Don Would you like to come home with me?

Lisa Only if you let me pay the check. (*Pause. He hands her the check. Blackout.*)

Scene Five

*Don's room. **Don** sits on the bed in his underwear, struggling to stay awake. **Phil** is asleep in a chair, head hanging back. **Jack** stands over him, watching.*

Jack   Don. (*Louder.*) Don. Come here.

Don   What is it?

Jack   You gotta see this. Come here. Come *on.* (**Don** *gets up.*) Quiet, quiet . . . (**Don** *joins* **Jack**.) Look at him. (**Don** *looks at* **Phil**.)

Don   So?

Jack   Look at his eyes. (**Don** *looks at* **Phil** *more closely. Pause.*)

Don   Oh man.

Jack   What did I tell you?

Don   That is *weird.* His *eyes* are open.

Jack   It was all the talk of Boys' Bunk Twelve.

Don   You sure he can't see us? (**Jack** *wriggles his fingers in front of* **Phil**'s *face.*) How can he sleep like that? I mean . . .

Jack   I know. It's a very disturbing concept.

Don   Yeah, it sure is. (*Pause.* **Don** *yawns.* **Jack** *lights up a joint.*)

Jack   So, Don, you vicious party beast, what's up next in our parade of pleasure?

Don   I don't know.

Jack   Twisted sex? Substance abuse? Senseless acts of violence?

Don   Maybe we should pack it in.

Jack   *What?*

Don   Well . . .

Jack   You didn't *mean* that.

Don   That's right, I didn't.

Jack   No, what we're going to *do* is, we're going to have a contest.

Don   Why not.

Jack   I want you to reach back, Don, deep into that ravaged brain of yours, I want you to think hard and tell me . . . three things that happened in the nineteen-seventies. (*Pause.*)

Don   We already did that, Jack.

Jack   We did?

Don   We did that one like a month ago.

Jack   Oh. (*Pause.*) Did we enjoy it?

Phil (*in his sleep*)   Mom, I'm home.

Don   What?

Jack   Oh, this is great, he's talking in his sleep.

Don   Makes two of us.

Jack   Phil's really a fascinating guy when he's unconscious. Living next door to him expanded my horizons. (*In* **Phil**'s *ear*.) Philip, this is your mother.

Phil   Mom . . .

Jack   I have something to tell you. You're not really our son. You're adopted.

Don   Hey, don't do that.

Jack   We found you in the hold of a Lebanese freighter . . .

Don   Jack, leave him alone.

Jack   Gosh, Mrs Cleaver, Theodore and I were only playing.

Don   You might be doing something to him.

Jack   Not Phil. He's got an iron constitution.

Don   You treat him like that when you guys were growing up?

Jack   Yes, as a matter of fact.

Don   You ever think he might not like it?

Jack   I always assumed he'd be grateful for the attention. I know I would be. (*Pause.*) Anything on the tube?

Don   There's a guide thing under the clothes there.

Jack   You expect me to touch those?

Don   It's clean, I just haven't folded it yet. Hey, come on, don't start throwing everything around. It's not in the books –

Jack (*picking up a paperback*)   *Clans of the Alphane Moon.* Spaceships, how can you read this stuff?

Don   I like it.

Jack (*reading the back*)   'A planet of madmen was the key to Earth's survival!'

Don (*reaching for it*)   Come on, Jack, put it down.

Jack (*opening a page at random*)   'His efforts to make a sensible equation out of the situation – '

Don   Jack, come on –

Jack   ' – out of the situation – '

Don   Jack –

Jack   ' – the situation had borne fruit – '

Don   You're *bending* the *cover*! (*Pause.*)

Jack (*dropping the book*)   Nothing personal, Don, but you're one of the most anal slobs I know.

Don   Thank you.

Jack I mean, it was fine when we lived like this in *college* . . . (*He finds the listings.*) Here we are. Let's see, we got, hmm, 'Famine '88' . . . 'World at War' . . . whoa, tits and car crashes on HBO!

Don I don't get cable.

Jack *What?* Are you serious?

Don I'm not paying to watch TV.

Jack You gotta get cable, Don. You're showing your age around here.

Don *Okay*, boss.

Phil (*in his sleep*) It's like your tongue. (*They both look at* **Phil**. *He rolls over. The alarm clock rings.* **Don** *shuts it off. Pause.*)

Don Time to get up.

Jack Working the night shift?

Don Guess I set it wrong.

Jack Don, let me ask you a question.

Don Uhm.

Jack Every time I come here, you're always in your underwear.

Don So?

Jack Don't you own any pants?

Don I like to be prepared.

Jack For what?

Don Going to sleep.

Jack Are we hinting at something?

Don Forget it.

Jack Hey, if you want me to go don't just sit there in your shorts in*sinu*ating. Just tell me. Look me in the eye and say, Listen here Jack, I'm sorry, it's late, I can *see* you've got *things* on your *mind* but I'd rather go to sleep than sit here in my ratty underwear listening to you. Be honest, Don. Don't get all *ironic* for fuck's sake. Keep me away from irony.

Don   Now listen here, Jack . . .

Jack   Yes?

Don   Have another beer. (*He hands* **Jack** *a beer.*)

Jack   Thank you. (*He opens it but does not drink. Pause.*)

Don   So what's on your mind?

Jack   Did I say something was on my mind?

Don   You hinted at it ironically.

Jack   Don, if you knew anything about me at all, you'd know this: Nothing ever bothers me.

Don   You're lucky that way.

Jack   Luck's got nothing to do with it. It's a matter of style. Imagine. You have a problem, just ask yourself one simple question: What would Ray Charles do in a situation like this? And Ray, I think, hipster that he is –

Don   What problem?

Jack   *The* problem, whatever problem you're *talking* about, I don't know. But Ray, Badass *Ray* –

Phil   I don't know, is this my house?

Jack   Fucking myna bird in a sport coat here.

Don   What problems.

Jack   You heard the latest? This girl, he's been seeing her a week, every night he goes to her place, right, they talk about the whales or something, he gets to sleep on the couch. She says she's frigid. He says it doesn't matter. She says her uncle raped her when she was ten. He says I love you. She says maybe you shouldn't come by any more. He says let's give it time. She says I'm screwing somebody else. He says it's all right, we can work around it. Isn't that so *typical*?

Don   Poor guy.

Jack   Calls me up, he says Jack, listen, I'm scared to be alone tonight –

Don   When?

Jack   This, tonight. What am I gonna do, say no? I mean, a friend's a friend. No matter how you look at it. (*Pause. Lowering his voice.*) But I'll tell you something about Phil.

Don   Yeah?

Jack   He's a homo.

Don   What?

Jack   Gay as a coot.

Don   Are you kidding? He told you?

Jack   No he didn't *tell* me, he doesn't even know it.

Don   How do you know it?

Jack   Don, look at the women he goes with. They eat Kal Kan for breakfast. And *they* all dump *him*. That's not normal.

Don   Is this for real?

Jack   Look at the facts. (*Pause.*)

Don   Well . . . so?

Jack   *So?*

Don   So he's you know, so what? (*Pause.*)

Jack   Exactly, so what?

Don   I mean in this day and age . . .

Jack   At this point in time, yes, Don, I know what you're saying, you're right, absolutely right. Absolutely.

Don   So what are we *arguing*?

Jack   We're not arguing, we're discussing.

Don   What are we discussing?

Jack   We're not discussing anything. (*Pause.*)

Don   Won't your wife be worried?

Jack   About what?

Don   Where you are.

Jack   Nah. Actually . . . actually she's out of town right now.

Don   Is she?

Jack   Her bank sent her out there, out to, ah, Ohio. Gonna finance another goddamn shopping mall.

Don   She must be doing pretty well, they trust her with that.

Jack   Somebody's gotta put bread on the table.

Don   You guys have a great arrangement.

Jack   I thank Jesus every day. (*Pause.*)

Don   So who's taking care of Jason?

Jack   Well, he's out there with her.

Don   Out there in Ohio.

Jack   It's the kind of place you want to see when you're young.

Don   Sure.

Jack   They'll be back pretty soon.

Don   Yeah. (*Pause.*)

Jack   How's your sex life, Don?

Don   Well, you know.

Jack I don't know, that's why I'm asking.

Don It's fine, I'm seeing this girl.

Jack Well well.

Don Yeah.

Jack Well well *well*. What's she like?

Don She's ah . . . she's sort of . . . I guess she's kind of serious. You know? Very . . . thoughtful. We talk a lot.

Jack I bet.

Don No, it's . . . she's always asking me questions. Why do I do this, do I say that . . . we talk about how we feel, about things, and . . . I'm learning to be responsible . . . and, ah . . .

Jack Tits?

Don They're okay.

Jack Hmm. Well, I wish you luck. (*Pause.*)

Don Actually she may be coming over a little later.

Jack A *little* later? It's fucking three in the morning.

Don She's a waitress over by the park, finishes at four.

Jack Sounds pretty devoted.

Don Well.

Jack So why you been keeping her a secret?

Don She's not a secret, she's . . . you know . . .

Jack A waitress.

Don She's really a sculptor.

Jack Does she get paid for that?

Don Not yet, no.

Jack Is she in a *museum*?

Don She just started . . .

Jack   So she's a dabbler, right? She's a waitress who
dabbles, nothing to be ashamed of. Why don't you say that,
does it embarrass you?

Don   No . . .

Jack   Really? (*He rubs his face.* **Phil** *mutters in his sleep.*) Hey,
you wanna go bowling? That's right, you can't.

Don   What did you mean by that?

Jack   Bowling. Duck pins. Sport of Kings.

Don   About being a waitress.

Jack   Huh? I don't know, that's what she is, right? I
didn't mean anything. You wanna go?

Don   It was insulting, Jack.

Jack   I didn't mean it to be.

Don   No, okay, you didn't, but it was. You do that all the
time.

Jack   What's this about?

Don   Listen, you could be a little more considerate, all
right?

Jack   What am I, your therapist?

Don   Jesus, you're doing it again!

Jack   What?

Don   You're insulting me!

Jack   Oh come on, don't be an asshole.

Don   *Stop* it!

Jack   I'm not doing anything, Don. Why are you getting
so excited? Are you under orders? This is not like you.
She's a waitress, she's a sculptress, fuck do I care I never
even *met* her, tell me –

Don   I feel you really –

Jack   You *feel*, everybody *feels*, *fuck* that. What are you, are you a man? Can't you control yourself? You're *opening up*. You're being *sensitive*. That's a nice *trick*, Don. But don't let it go to your head or you'll wind up getting yanked around by the wiener. (*Pause.*) As they say in the vernacular.

Don   I am not getting 'yanked around'.

Jack   I didn't say you were, I merely –

Don   Then take it back.

Jack   Okay, I hit a sore spot –

Don   Take it back.

Jack   Please, don't *be* this way –

Don   Take it back! (*Pause.*)

Jack   All right, Don. Shhh. All right. This is childish. Be cool. Be *cool*. It's me, remember? Not some lady you're trying to bring home. We *know* each other. We know what we really are. We're men, Don. We do terrible things. Let's admit we like them and start from there. You want to be a different person? Get a hug, all the bad thoughts disappear? I'm sorry, it won't *work* that way. It's not like changing your shirt, we can't *promise* to be better. That's a lie. What do you want, Don? Be honest. Do what you *want*. Please. I beg you. Because if you don't, what kind of ma . . . what are you gonna be then? (**Don** *says nothing.*) I am your friend, Don. I care about you. I really do. Okay? (**Don** *says nothing.*) So you wanna go bowling? Hey, I got some amyl, you wanna do amyl? Don?

Phil   All my shoes . . . line 'em up . . .

Jack (*to* **Don**)   What you want, Don. Just think about it. (*Pause.*)

Don   Yeah.

Jack (*poking* **Phil**)   Phil, wake up, we gotta go. (**Phil** *rolls over.* **Jack** *looks at him. To* **Don**.) Hey, you wanna see something? You'll get a kick out of this, it's up your alley.

(*He hands* **Don** *a piece of notepaper with crayon markings on it.*)
Jason left that. Go ahead, read it aloud.

Don   'Dear Daddy, Mommy is taking me on jet. We are
going to planet light blue. It has a river, and some caves
called feeling caves, a waterfall, beds, and slides. There is a
city there called "girls are for you". I know that is true. I
love you but I think I am going to stay here.' (*Pause.*)
Sounds better than Ohio.

Jack   Yeah right. (*Pause.*) You know, I read that and I
thought . . . what the fuck does this mean? Is he insane?
What is going on inside this kid's head? I watch him, right,
he's this tiny guy, really, his sneakers are like this big . . .
but something's going on in there. Something's going on.
(*Pause.*) When he was born, did I tell you this? . . . He –

Don (*handing back the note*)   She's an artist, Jack. Not a
waitress. Understand? (*Pause.*)

Jack   Yes, Don. Of course. Thank you. I'm glad we could
have this little moment together. Only listen, Don . . .
(*Pause.*) Don't forget who your friends are. (*He leans into*
Phil*'s ear.*) *Phil.*

Phil   Huh?

Jack   Time to go home.

Phil   Go?

Jack   Come on.

Phil   Fell asleep.

Jack   No kidding. (*A knock on the door.*)

Don (*getting up*)   Oh Jesus.

Phil   Feel rotten. (**Don** *meets* **Lisa** *at the door and blocks her*
entrance.)

Lisa   Hi.

Don   You're early.

Lisa   You're right. Nice legs.

Phil   I'm never looking at another woman again.

Jack   Very practical.

Lisa   What's going on?

Don   Some friends came by.

Phil   I've done bad things, Jack. So many bad things.

Lisa   Sorry to disturb you.

Don   Don't start.

Lisa   I only ran over here in the middle of the night.

Jack (*singing*)   'Well, I used to be disgusted . . .'

Lisa   Are you going to introduce us?

Don   Guys, this is Lisa. Lisa, this is Jack. That's Phil. He sleeps with his eyes open.

Jack   Young Theodore is afraid of the dark.

Lisa   Excuse me?

Jack   I said he's afraid of the dark.

Lisa   I thought his name was Phil.

Jack   I was making a joke.

Lisa   Why?

Jack   In order to be funny.

Lisa   Well. So you're the funny one.

Jack   Have we met before?

Lisa   No. But we know who we are.

Don   You want me to call you a cab? Jack? (**Jack** *walks up to* **Lisa**. *He puts his arm around* **Don**. *He smiles.*)

Jack   Don tells me you're a very talented sculptress. (*Blackout.*)

Scene Six

The park. **Jack** *and* **Phil** *sitting on a bench.* **Jack** *with a child's toy in his hand.* **Phil** *looking out front.*

Phil   I would have destroyed myself for this woman.
Gladly. I would have eaten garbage. I would have sliced
my *wrists* open. Under the right circumstances, I mean, if
she said, 'Hey, Phil, why don't you just cut your wrists
open,' well, come on, but if *seriously* . . . We clicked, we
connected on so many things, right off the bat, we talked
about God for *three hours* once, I don't know what good it
did, but that *intensity* . . . and the first time we went to bed,
I didn't even touch her. I didn't *want* to, understand what
I'm saying? And you know, I played it very casually,
because, all right, I've had some rough experiences, I'm the
first to admit, but after a couple of weeks I could feel we
were right there, so I laid it down, everything I wanted to
tell her, and . . . and she says to me . . . she says . . .
'Nobody should ever need another person that badly.' Do
you *believe* that? 'Nobody should ever . . .'! What is that? Is
that something you saw on TV? I dump my *heart* on the
table, you give me Joyce Dr Fucking Brothers? 'Need,
need,' I'm saying I *love* you, is that wrong? Is that not
allowed any more? (*Pause.* **Jack** *looks at him.*) And so what if
I did need her? Is that so bad? All right, crucify me, I
needed her! So *what!* I don't want to be by myself, I'm by
myself I feel like I'm going out of my mind, I do. I sit
there, I'm thinking forget it, I'm not gonna make it through
the next *ten seconds*, I just can't *stand* it. But I do, somehow,
I get through the ten seconds, but then I have to do it all
over again, 'cause they just keep coming, all these . . .
seconds, floating by, while I'm waiting for something to
happen, I don't know what, a car wreck, a nuclear war or
something, that sounds awful but at least there'd be this
instant when I'd know I was alive. Just once. 'Cause I look
in the mirror, and I can't believe I'm really there. I can't
believe that's me. It's like my body, right, is the size of,
what, the Statue of Liberty, and I'm inside it, I'm down in
one of the legs, this gigantic hairy leg, I'm scraping around

inside my own foot like some tiny foetus. And I don't know who I am, or where I'm going. And I wish I'd never been born. (*Pause.*) Not only that, my hair is falling out, and that really *sucks*. (*Pause.*)

Jack You know, Phil, in Cambodia . . . they don't have *time* to worry about things like that.

Phil Maybe I'll move there.

Jack Well, keep in touch.

Phil Or maybe I'll just kill myself.

Jack Hmm. (*Pause.*) Hey, Phil.

Phil What.

Jack Let's see that smile.

Phil Leave me alone.

Jack Ah, come on.

Phil Get *away*.

Jack Come on, Phil, I see it, I see that smile, come on, come *on*, ooo, here it comes –

Phil I'm not *gonna*.

Jack Yes you are, come on, just a little, just a weensy, just an unsey bunsey, just a meensee neensee, just a –

Phil All right, God damn it! I'm smiling, okay? I'm happy, oh I'm so *happy*, ha ha ha! I hate when you do this.

Jack One day you'll miss me, Phil.

Phil Probably. (*Pause. He looks out.*) Well, Jason seems to be enjoying himself.

Jack Why wouldn't he be?

Phil I don't know. He just seems . . . glad to be back.

Jack I don't see what you're getting at.

Phil   I'm just saying it's . . . good that . . . you and Carla
. . . worked it out.

Jack   Worked what out?

Phil   Whatever it was. Between you.

Jack   There was nothing 'between' us, Phil.

Phil   Oh. Okay.

Jack   If there *was* something 'between' us, we'd sit down
and discuss it like reasonable adults. We'd come to an
agreement. We'd draw up certain rules, and then we'd
follow them. Our feelings don't have to enter *into* it. (*Pause.*)

Phil   Well, she's a lovely girl, Jack.

Jack   She is, Phil. She certainly is. And I'm the luckiest
palooka. (*Pause.*) So . . . you heard from Don lately?

Phil   No. What's he up to?

Jack   That's what I'm asking you.

Phil   I don't know, he doesn't call me. Why would he call
me?

Jack   He might be trying to get in touch with me.

Phil   Why wouldn't he just call *you*?

Jack   Well, maybe he *has*, but I've been busy, Phil. I
don't have time to sit around staring at the phone. I have
things to do. I have food to eat and records to play. I've got
places I have to be at and then come back from. I've got
miles to go before I sleep. *All* sorts of stuff. (*Pause.*) Darn it,
who needs him? Let him play with his dolls. We're having
a heck of a time all by ourselves, aren't we little fella?

Phil   I guess.

Jack   Ho, you bet we *are*. (*Pause.*) You *bet* we are. (*Pause.*)
You know, Phil, what was the biggest mistake we ever
made in our lives?

Phil   What? (**Maggie** *enters, in running gear.* **Jack** *sees her. Pause.*)

Jack (*to* **Phil**)   What?

Phil   You were gonna say –

Jack   Was I? (*To* **Maggie**.) That's our face!

Maggie (*seeing him*)   Well, hello.

Jack   Miss, I've never seen you before, but how would you like to be a star?

Phil   Jack . . .

Maggie   Might be fun.

Jack   *Fun?* My friend here is too shy to mention it, but he happens to be the associate producer of a new major motion picture. And frankly you've just saved him a trip across the continent. (*To* **Phil**.) Go ahead, tell her about the picture.

Phil   I, ah . . . um . . .

Jack   The picture is a modern picture. It's an American picture. It's the modern story of American men and their modern American women, set against a backdrop as modern and American as all indoors. It's a spectacle, it's an epic, it's the story of a generation that had it all and couldn't figure out what to do with it. And it's the story of a girl, one special girl, and her quest for meaning in a world she never made. And of the man who wouldn't rest until he tracked her down.

Maggie   Why would he do that?

Jack   He couldn't think of anything better to do.

Maggie   Sounds stupid.

Jack   That's what I say. I keep telling him to make a teenage sex farce, but does he listen? (*To* **Phil**.) Do you listen?

Phil   What?

Jack   He never listens!

Maggie   How's your ward?

Jack   Discreet as ever.

Maggie   Good to know.

Jack   How's life at the waxworks?

Maggie   Don't ask me.

Jack   Believe me, I won't. (*Pause.*)

Maggie   Mind if I sit?

Jack   Mind if she sits?

Phil   No ... I –

Jack   We don't mind if you sit. (**Maggie** *sits between* **Jack** *and* **Phil**. *Pause.*)

Phil   My name's Phil, by the way.

Maggie   Hello, Phil.

Phil   This is my friend Jack.

Maggie (*laughing*)   Hello, Jack. (**Jack** *nods.*)

Phil   You two know each other?

Maggie   Do we know each other?

Jack   We don't know each other.

Phil   Oh.

Maggie   Ever feel you're about to do something you're really going to regret?

Jack   Never. (*Pause.*)

Phil   Well, hey ... so you been out doing some *running*, huh? (**Maggie** *and* **Jack** *look at each other. They smile. Blackout.*)

Scene Seven

Lights up. **Don** *and a* **Girl** *in bed. Night. A lit candle sits in a saucer.*

Girl   Something is coming to get me. I've never seen it, but I know it's there. It thinks about me all the time. One night I'll wake up for no reason and it will be with me. And in that moment I will realize that this is my last minute on Earth. (*Pause.*) Are you still up?

Don   Yeah.

Girl   I have visions. I close my eyes and see things. There's nothing I can do about it. Once I closed my eyes and I saw a plane going down in a jungle. Inside a boy and girl were sucking on an orange. Their bodies were eaten by monkeys. Another time I saw an old man sitting on a porch. He had just put pomade in his hair. He said, Mike, clean that blade and stick it in the garage. I have no idea what that was about at all.

Don   You saw this?

Girl   I didn't *see* it, but I *saw* it. You know? (*Pause.*)

Don   Do you like working in the record store?

Girl   I don't work in a record store.

Don   I bought a record from you.

Girl   I was only pretending to work there. I do that sometimes, go into a place and pretend to work there.

Don   Why?

Girl   I'm mentally ill.

Don   Oh.

Girl   Does that disturb you?

Don   It depends.

Girl   On what?

Don   Whether it's true or not.

Girl   I used to be a lot worse. When I was fourteen I weighed eighty pounds. I didn't eat. I was trying to make myself disappear. Getting rid of my flesh seemed easy. But I couldn't figure out how to get rid of my bones. That's the hardest part.

Don   I imagine it would be.

Girl   You don't believe me, do you?

Don   I didn't say that.

Girl   What would you think if I told you my father tried to run me over with a steamroller?

Don   Hmm ... well ...

Girl   He was a daredevil. There were six capes in his closet. I was part of the act. He would tie me up and put me in a laundry bag. Then he would come at me in a steamroller. I had thirty seconds to escape. What you have to do is totally relax your muscles. Then the cords slip right off. But my father would tie double knots.

Don   Why?

Girl   He wanted to kill me.

Don   Why did he want to do that?

Girl   Because he wasn't allowed to fuck me. (*Silence.* **Don** *looks uncomfortable. Suddenly he gets out of bed and reaches for his shirt.*) What's wrong?

Don   Nothing. Excuse me.

Girl   Where are you going?

Don   Out. Don't worry. I just have to go. Uh, listen, the front door locks itself so just slam it on your way out.

Girl   I don't understand, you're leaving?

Don   I think I ... um, there's some Hi-C in the fridge, help yourself, okay, and I'll, we'll talk later ...

Girl   Have I upset you?

Don   No, no . . .

Girl   Was it something I said?

Don   Look, I'm sorry, it was nice meeting you, but I don't think . . . you and I should . . .

Girl   Don't you like me?

Don   It's not a question of that –

Girl   What did I do wrong?

Don   Nothing. Really.

Girl   Please, ah . . . please, come here. I know I'm strange. I can't help it . . . Listen, I can tell fortunes. Did you know that? I can. Would you let me tell your fortune?

Don   What?

Girl   Give me your hand. Please? I know this is upsetting you. I can't help it. Just give me your hand. Then you can go. (*Pause.*) Please? (*Pause.* **Don** *gives her his hand.*) There, yes. That's better. This is very good. Now . . . calm yourself. Clear your mind. Yes . . . yes. Are you relaxed? Nod your head. (**Don** *nods his head.*) Ah, yes. This is the hand of a man. Very strong. Very powerful. This is a hand that will perform great acts. Terrible, but great. It will hurt many people. But it will seldom be raised in anger. It is the hand of a compassionate man. A man with a large soul. (*Pause.*) Should I go on?

Don   Okay.

Girl   You feel that you have yet to live. That the years are passing like a dream. This is true. But soon all that will change. People will flock to you. Men . . .

Don   Women?

Girl   Women, yes. They will be drawn to you. To your power. It cannot be hidden. (*Pause.*)

Don   How will I die?

Girl   At sea. When you are very old. Your body will never be found. (*Pause.*)

Don   You're scaring the shit out of me.

Girl   Everything will be all right.

Don   Do you work in the record store or not?

Girl   It doesn't matter. Come here.

Don   I'm not going to be able to see you again . . .

Girl   Yes.

Don   I shouldn't be doing this . . . I'm gonna get in trouble . . .

Girl   A man can do anything he wants. I'm blowing out the candle now. Are you going to stay?

Don   Well . . .

Girl   Then come to bed. (**Don** *gets into bed. Pause.*)

Don   Are any of the things you told me true?

Girl   They're true if you think they're true. (*Pause.*)

Don   Do *you* think they're true? (*The* **Girl** *looks at* **Don**. *Pause. She blows out the candle. Blackout.*)

Scene Eight

Lights up on **Don**'s *room.* **Lisa** *stands,* **Don** *sits on the edge of the bed. They are both in their underwear.* **Lisa** *holds a pair of panties. Silence.*

Lisa   And that's all you have to say about it?

Don   What else do you want me to say?

Lisa   How about sorry?

Don   Well, of course I'm sorry. How could I not be sorry?

Lisa   You haven't *said* it.

Don   I'm sorry.

Lisa   No you're not. (*Pause.*) I'm going. (*She starts gathering her clothes.*)

Don   Um –

Lisa   What?

Don   I, ah –

Lisa   YES? WHAT? WHAT IS IT?

Don   I just think you should realize that I've been under a lot of strain lately.

Lisa   I see.

Don   And maybe, I've, you know, handled some things badly –

Lisa   You're under a lot of strain so you go off and fuck somebody else.

Don   That's unnecessarily blunt.

Lisa   Christ but you're a cheeky bastard. Couldn't you even bother to clean up before I came? Put away the odd pair of panties?

Don   I thought they were yours.

Lisa   I don't buy my panties at *Job* Lot, Don. And I have a low opinion of people who do. (*She throws the panties at him. He fools with them and puts them over his head like a cap.*)

Don   They keep your ears warm.

Lisa   You think I'm kidding, don't you? You think, well, Lisa's just having a little *episode*, it'll all blow over, chalk it up to boyish exuberance, hit the sack? Who the fuck do you think you are, James Bond? (*Pause.*) Did you use a condom?

Don   Huh?

Lisa   A *condom*. You know what they are. You see them on TV all the time.

Don   Wha – why?

Lisa   Because you slept with her, and then you slept with me, and you don't know who she's been fucking, do you, *Don*. DO YOU. (*Pause.*) I'm going.

Don   Where?

Lisa   I'm going to lie down in traffic, Don. I'm going to let a crosstown bus roll over me because my life is meaningless since you betrayed me. I'm going to my *apartment*, you stupid shithead!

Don   Lisa, it was just a very casual thing. It's over.

Lisa   What do I care?

Don   I made a mistake, I admit that, but . . .

Lisa   But what?

Don   It made me realize something, something very important.

Lisa   Yes?

Don   (*very softly*)   I love you.

Lisa   What? I can't hear you.

Don   I said I –

Lisa   I *heard* what you said! 'You love me'! That doesn't mean shit! This isn't high school, I'm wearing your *pin*. You want me to tell you what really counts? Out here with the graduates?

Don   What?

Lisa   It's not worth it! Do what you want, it doesn't matter to me. I don't even know you, Don. After four months I don't know who you are or why you do what you do. You keep getting your dick stuck in things. What is that all about, anyway? Will someone please explain that to me?

(*Pause.*) Don't look at me that way.

Don   What way?

Lisa   Like a whipped dog. It's just pathetic.

Don   Lisa, please. I did something very stupid. I won't do it again.

Lisa   Do you have any idea what you're saying?

Don   I'm saying I feel bad.

Lisa   I'm sorry, but 'I feel bad' isn't even in the running. Not at all. We're talking about faith. *Semper fidelis*, like the Marines. They don't leave people lying in foxholes. They just do it. They don't 'feel bad'.

Don   How do you know so much about the Marines?

Lisa   It's not the Marines, Don. It's got nothing to do with the fucking Marines. It's the idea. (*Pause.*) You don't understand what I'm talking about, do you? You're just afraid of being punished. I'm not you're *mother*. I don't spank. (*Pause.*) I'm going. Have fun fucking your bargain shopper and cracking jokes with your creepy friends.

Don   Lisa, wait, I have to tell you something.

Lisa   No you don't.

Don   I had this dream about you last night.

Lisa   How inconvenient.

Don   Can I tell you this? Just for a minute? Please? (*Pause.*)

Lisa   *Start.*

Don   Okay ... okay ... now ... I was ... flying. In a plane, I mean a rocket. It was a rocket ship. And I was all alone inside. With nothing to eat but junk food in rocks along the walls – sandwich cremes. Raisinets, boxes and boxes of crap. The smell was nauseating.

Lisa   Does this go on much longer?

Don Anyway I looked outside and there was this tiny planet floating by me like a blue Nerf ball. So I opened a bottle of Yoohoo and sat down to relax. But it must have been doped because it knocked me right out. When I woke up . . . the cabin was on fire! I tried to move but someone had tied me to the chair with piano wire, it was slicing into my wrists like they were chunks of ham. The ship was in a nose-dive and I was slammed against the seat. Suddenly, bam, the whole port side blew away. I could see the planet rolling beneath me. A new world, Lisa. Pristine, unsullied. Virgin. I reached out . . . and the ship broke up around me in a sheet of flames. I was tied to a chair falling through the void. My mind left me. (*Pause.*) When I came to I was lying on a beach half buried in the sand. My right hand was gone. The wire had severed it at the wrist. Leeches sucked on the stump. I rolled over and waited for death. And then . . . you rose from the water on a bed of seaweed. On the white sands your hips swayed with an animal rhythm. I don't know why you were there. I didn't ask. You knelt down and gave me nectar from a gourd. You healed me in the shade of the trees. And you never spoke. And neither did I. I had forgotten how. Later on we built a shelter. You bore many children while I caught fish with a spear in the blue light of three moons. And then, one day, we lay ourselves down together on the sand. The breath eased from our bodies. And we died. And the ocean ate our bones. (*Pause.*)

Lisa What a crock of shit. You expect me to believe that?

Don It's true. I dreamt it.

Lisa You've got a vivid imagination. I'll grant you that much. Very . . . charming. Very romantic.

Don It's an omen. It's like a prophecy.

Lisa Of what?

Don Of us. The two of us, together.

Lisa Well. (*Pause.*) You'd probably make me do the fishing.

Don I wouldn't. I promise. (*Pause.*)

Lisa Wait. Wait. This is not it. This is nothing. I can't even talk to you until you tell me the truth. Why did you do this, Don? When you knew I trusted you? Was it her breasts, her buttocks, the smell of her sweat? Was it her underwear? Was it because she wasn't me? Did you have a reason? Any reason at all?

Don I wanted to see . . . if I could get away with it.

Lisa Why?

Don Because that's what a man would do. (*Pause.*) Let's get married, Lisa. I want to marry you. I want to be faithful to you for ever. I want to put my head on your lap. Can I do that? I want to bury my face in your lap. I don't want to think about anything. Is that okay? (*Pause.*)

Lisa Would you like to play a little game, Don?

Don What kind of game?

Lisa A pretend game. Let's pretend you could do anything you wanted to. And whatever you did, nobody could blame you for it. Not me or anyone else. You would be totally free. You wouldn't have to make promises and you wouldn't have to lie. All you would have to do is know how you feel. Just that. How would that be?

Don I don't know.

Lisa Just pretend. What would you do? (*Pause.*)

Don I think I would be . . . different?

Lisa Would you?

Don I'd like to be.

Lisa Different how? (*Pause.*)

Don Well . . . I would . . . I think I would . . . I think maybe I . . . (*He pauses and falls into a long silence. Blackout.*)

Scene Nine

In the blackout, the **bandleader**'s *voice.*

Bandleader   All right, everybody, before you get *too* comfortable in your chairs, let's see if we can work off a little of that delicious roast beef with some of today's young sounds. (*A small, accordion-led combo strikes up with 'Beat It'. Lights up on* **Phil** *and* **Jack** *seated at a round banquet table littered with napkins, glasses, and half-eaten dinners.* **Jack** *has a row of soda-filled glasses lined up in front of him. He methodically pours sugar into them one by one, watching as they foam up explosively.* **Phil** *stares straight ahead.*)

Phil (*after a while*)   Christ, I hate weddings. They're so depressing, you know? They remind me of funerals.

Jack   Weddings remind you of funerals?

Phil   They remind me of death.

Jack   Everything reminds you of death, Phil.

Phil   No it doesn't.

Jack   What are you thinking about right now?

Phil   Well, I'm thinking about death. But only because you brought it up.

Jack   I didn't bring it up, you brought it up.

Phil   No I didn't.

Jack   You said you hate weddings because they remind you of death.

Phil   People are drinking those, you know.

Jack   Not any more.

Phil   That is so childish, Jack.

Jack   Is it?

Phil   You don't think so?

Jack   Well . . . (*He pauses and bursts out laughing.*)

Phil   Why don't you grow up?

Jack   You need some more dope. You'll feel better.

Phil   I don't *want* to feel better. I wish I was dead.

Jack   You gotten laid lately, Phil?

Phil   What do you care?

Jack   I like to know my friends are happy.

Phil   I think that's incredibly tactless.

Jack   Well, I'm sorry you see it that way. (*Pause.*) So you *haven't* gotten laid?

Phil   You're so curious, yes, yes, I have *gotten laid*, is that okay?

Jack   Yes, that's fine. (*Pause.*)

Phil   You don't have any idea what it's like, Jack. You're completely out of it. You've got your wife and your kid. You've got stability. You don't have to make yourself crawl through the gutter to get regular sex. When I think of some of the things I've done . . . it just makes me feel sick. (*Pause.*)

Jack   Like for instance?

Phil   Oh, please.

Jack   No, I mean what things?

Phil   I'm not here to provide you with titillation.

Jack   Yes you are, Phil. You just don't know it. (*Pause. Out front.*) There she goes, the old Earth Mother . . . Hi, Honey! No, we're doing fine, we're dandy . . . Look at her, she's plastered across the walls. One drink and she's ready for pearl diving without a loincloth. She won't keep booze in the house, you know. Jason might invite some nursery buddies in for an afternoon mixer. Not to mention she wants the VCR disconnected, she thinks he needs *more creative* playtime so she bought these toys from Scandinavia, and you know what they are, they're unpainted blocks of wood, you're supposed to have fun *arranging* them. You look at these things and you know why the Swedes keep offing themselves. So I tell her –

Phil If you must know, I fucked a girl while she was unconscious.

Jack Beg pardon?

Phil You want to know so I'm telling you!

Jack You . . . fucked a girl while she was . . . unconscious?

Phil Yes.

Jack How?

Phil I deserve to die.

Jack I'll decide that, Phil. Just what have you done?

Phil I didn't *do* anything. She blinked off.

Jack When? Where?

Phil We went out, we came back to her place –

Jack Who is this?

Phil You don't know her.

Jack What does she look like?

Phil You don't *know* her.

Jack Did she have nice tits? Just tell me about the tits.

Phil It doesn't *matter*.

Jack Just tell me!

Phil They were okay.

Jack Only okay?

Phil No, they were fine.

Jack Good. Go on.

Phil So we came back to her place, one of these

subdivided closets, right, and the radiators are howling. It was like a pizza oven in there. She pours a couple of Scotches, we talk a little. Pretty soon I can tell I won't be coming home tonight.

Jack   You bounder.

Phil   So I get her blouse off –

Jack   Wait, wait, how'd that happen?

Phil   Just, you know, in the course of conversation. It's time to make my move, I take her in my arms . . .

Jack   Uh-huh . . .

Phil   She keels right over. Wham. Right down on the futon.

Jack   Geez.

Phil   I'm telling you it was *hot* in there.

Jack   I guess so.

Phil   Anyway, I tried to bring her around, but she'd had a lot to drink, you should have seen the liquor tab, luckily I was able to charge it – so I thought, isn't this great, this is just the way I want to spend my evening. I was pretty pissed off.

Jack   So you fucked her anyway, huh?

Phil   No! What do you think I am? . . . I decided to put her to bed. I'd sleep on the floor and keep an eye on her. So, I did that, but she was sweating so much, it looked un*healthy*, so I, ah . . .

Jack   You undressed her, right?

Phil   I took her shoes off, that's all! I took off her shoes, and she had on these tights, so I thought I better take those off too . . .

Jack   And then you fucked her.

Phil   I had her undressed and I thought, what the hell, I don't want to sleep on the floor, so I got into bed with her, and . . . I don't know. I don't know. I walked home afterwards, sixteen blocks at three in the morning. I was hoping somebody would kill me. I felt like . . . you know what's really terrifying? Everyone's worried about the world getting blown up or something, right, but . . . what if it doesn't? What if it just goes on like this, for ever? What are we gonna do then? (*Pause.*)

Jack   You sly old dog.

Phil   What?

Jack   What an operator, huh? You old dog.

Phil   I feel *awful*.

Jack   Ah, come on, Phil, drop the Hamlet routine. Did you speak to her yet?

Phil   Yeah. She called me. She said she was sorry she fell asleep and maybe we could go out again.

Jack   And nothing about . . .

Phil   No.

Jack   So? Everything's fine. You had a little fun, you covered your ass, and no one's the wiser. What's the problem? (*Pause.*)

Bandleader (*offstage*)   Don and Lisa, we wish you the very best of luck, life, and happiness. This song is just for you. (*The combo plays 'When I'm Sixty-four'.*)

Phil   What did you get them?

Jack   A blender. We had it lying around.

Phil   I wish I'd thought of that. I bought them a cheese wheel.

Jack   A what?

Phil   A cheese wheel. A wheel of cheese. It comes in the mail.

Jack   Uh-huh.

Phil   It's Yarlsberg. Most people like Yarlsberg, don't they?

Jack   I couldn't say, Phil. I know a lot but I don't know that.

Phil   What the hell, it's not like I see him every day. You catch the bride?

Jack   Yeah, she's a real bowzer, huh?

Phil   Jack . . .

Jack   What?

Phil   That's so rude.

Jack   Would you say that girl is attractive?

Phil   Your attitude towards women –

Jack   Hey, I don't have an *attitude* towards women. I'm not questioning her right to exist. I'm simply asking if you find her attractive.

Phil   No, I don't.

Jack   So why are you getting upset?

Phil   Maybe he loves her, did that ever occur to you?

Jack   Of course it *occurred* to me. I'm not an idiot. But that's not going to make her any better looking, is it? So don't give me this attitude bullshit, Phil. I'm just telling the truth. Nobody's going to punish you for telling the truth. (*Silence.* **Jack** *moves to pour sugar in* **Phil**'*s drink.*)

Phil   Don't do that.

Jack   I'm just *kidding.* (*Pause.*) Hey, you're still working at that place, aren't you?

Phil   Unfortunately.

Jack   Nine to five?

Phil   Uh-huh.

Jack   I want you to do me a favour.

Phil   Like what?

Jack   Like letting me use your apartment during the daytime.

Phil   Oh. Well, sure. Why not. (*Pause.*) How come?

Jack   Because I need to be able to be alone in the afternoons.

Phil   What's wrong with your apartment?

Jack   It's no good.

Phil   Why's that?

Jack   Why do you think?

Phil   I don't know.

Jack   You don't have to know, you just have to do me a favour.

Phil   It's my apartment, Jack. I'd like to know what it's being used for.

Jack   All right, don't do it. Jesus.

Phil   I mean I trust you, but –

Jack   Are you my friend?

Phil   Sure.

Jack   Then I need your help. I've got to meet somebody and I can't do it at my place.

Phil   A woman.

Jack   Yes. She is a woman.

Phil   I see.

Jack   You'll appreciate the difficulty.

Phil   Right.

Jack   So you'll do it?

Phil Um . . .

Jack Don't 'um', Phil, come on. I'd do it for you.

Phil That's a little different, isn't it? I mean . . . I'm
single. I'm supposed to do things like that. You're talking
about adultery.

Jack Oh, please.

Phil You and another woman, I don't know –

Jack Let's not get melodramatic. This has nothing to do
with adultery. This is just a nice little affair I'm going to let
myself have. A quick tour of foreign panties and then it's
back on the bus home. Everybody's happy and no one gets
hurt. What could be simpler?

Phil I don't think I can do it, Jack. I'd just feel too
guilty. I'd be helping you to ruin your life.

Jack You're joking, right?

Phil Did you tell this girl you're married?

Jack I've implied as much.

Phil But you haven't told her.

Jack Why am I having this discussion?

Phil You're so big on the truth, why didn't you tell her?

Jack Well, we're up on our little throne, are we? You
and your fucking sexual sob stories, you think you know the
answer?

Phil Yes, I do.

Jack No you don't. Absolutely not. You want to know
the *truth*, you want to know what I have *found out* while you
sit there twisting your guilt-ridden nuts off? *It doesn't matter!*
It doesn't *matter* what you do because nobody is watching,
Phil! Nobody's taking notes, nobody is heating up a
pitchfork, there *is* nobody there! So don't dare tell me that
I'm doing something wrong, because I decide that, and I
decide there *is* nothing wrong. I'm going to commit

adultery, Phil! I'm actually going against the Ten
Commandments, and as long as I'm careful and don't get
caught I don't give a shit. (*Pause.*) Nothing's happening,
Phil. Where's the lightning? (**Don** *enters in a tuxedo.*)

Don   We can't go on meeting like this.

Jack   Hey, here he is, the man of the minute.

Don   You two look like a couple of derelicts. How you
doing, Philly?

Phil   Okay, I'm great.

Jack   Put 'er there, Don. Big Don. Old Big Don.

Don   Why am I Big Don?

Jack   Because you are, that's why. You look like a waiter.
Here you go. (*He hands* **Don** *a gargantuan joint.*)

Don   Is this for real?

Jack   You can smoke some now and sublet the rest.

Phil   Congratulations, Don. I'm really happy for you.

Jack   Don't get maudlin, Phil.

Don   You guys having a good time?

Jack   You bet. I love eating next to the men's room.

Don   Huh? Oh, look, I'm really sorry about that . . .

Phil   Doesn't bother me . . .

Don   See, I didn't know, Lisa did the seating . . .

Jack   No need to apologize, Big Don. I'm sure you had
more important things on your mind.

Don   Well, yeah . . .

Jack   You couldn't be expected to bother with these little
details.

Don   I didn't look too stupid, did I?

Jack   No, not too stupid.

Don Did you notice when my collar button popped off?

Jack Actually, Big Don, I did not notice that. Actually I missed most of the ceremony, lovely as I know it must have been, actually since I was not part of the wedding party, that is the wedding party *per se*, I did not actually think it was that important for me to –

Phil Well, this is quite a reception. I love the, ah . . . and the *music* . . .

Don Yeah, Lisa's parents, they're very . . . you know, they wanted a big thing.

Jack And they're certainly getting a big thing, eh, Big Don?

Don Ho ho.

Jack Yep. (*Pause.*) So, Donerooney, this is the day for you, huh. Tying that wacky old knot. Strolling down that goofy aisle of matrimony. Setting down to a big heap o' domestic bliss.

Don Well, I hope so.

Jack You're gonna love it, kid. Take it from me. Be fruitful and multiply.

Phil She's a lovely girl, Don.

Don Huh?

Phil Lisa.

Don Well, thanks.

Jack Big Don, let me ask you something.

Don Shoot.

Jack You and the little woman, you're off on a honeymoon?

Don Uh-huh.

Jack So what's happening with your apartment while you're away?

Don   My folks are gonna stay there.

Jack   Well, isn't that thoughtful.

Don   Did you –

Jack   Me? Don't concern yourself with me. (*Pause.*)

Phil   Well, it's hard to believe.

Jack   What?

Phil   That we're here, all three of us. And that we've known each other, all these years. I mean we were younger, we didn't know what we were gonna do, or what was gonna happen and now we're all older, you've got a kid, you're getting married . . . just think.

Jack   It's not that difficult a concept, Phil.

Phil   I hope you and Lisa will be very happy together, Don.

Don   I don't see why not.

Jack   You can always get a divorce. (**Phil** *looks at him.*) What I say?

Phil   He just got *married*, Jack.

Jack   I'm aware of that. I'm just saying it's an option. It's something to take into account. Right, Don?

Don   Well, I suppose it's always a possibility.

Jack   You see? It's a possibility. (*Pause.*) You wanna smoke that reefer now?

Don   You have it. I'm not really supposed to.

Jack   Oh?

Don   I sort of promised myself. It's no big deal.

Jack   No, certainly not.

Don   It's something I've been wanting to do.

Jack   By all means.

Don   Anyway they're just as bad as cigarettes.

Jack   Yet another significant consideration. When do you learn to tie your shoes?

Don   I'm wearing slip-ons.

Jack   The bedrock of a lasting marriage.

Don (*casually*)   Fuck you, Jack.

Jack   Does that mean you don't love me any more?

Don   Not if you're gonna talk like that.

Jack   I thought we were discussing footwear. (*Pause.*)

Don   Jack, I'm sorry.

Jack   About what?

Don   I don't know.

Jack   Then why did you say it?

Don   I don't know, I thought . . . I don't know, I'm just sorry.

Jack   You know what I always like about you, Don? You're so fucking eager to please. It's really pathetic. (*Pause.*) In a zany kind of way. (*Pause.*)

Don   I better go. I have to wheel my aunt around.

Jack   Go get her, cowboy.

Don   I'm glad you guys came. I am. Listen, when I get back –

Jack   You know it.

Phil   Great.

Don   Okay. Rest easy. (*He exits. Pause.*)

Jack   Don of the Living Dead.

Phil   Huh?

Jack   Guy's walking around like a fucking *zombie*.

Phil   He looked all right to me.

Jack   Did he? Did he now?

Phil   He looked happy.

Jack   Phil, and I hate to be the one to break this to you, but you're hopelessly out of date. Happiness, that was the sixties. Paisley trousers, peace marches, that whole thing. This is the modern world. It's kinda young, kinda kooky, kinda –

Phil   Why don't you shut the fuck up. I'm sick of you and your miserable sarcastic bullshit. (*Pause.*) I'm gonna go dance the Hokey-Pokey.

Jack   Phil.

Phil   Don't say it.

Jack   No, Phil, wait, come here. Look at me, come on.

Phil   What?

Jack   This is bad. This is all wrong. I'm kidding, doesn't anybody know I'm kidding? Look at me, do I look serious?

Phil   No.

Jack   No, of course not, no, how long do we know each other?

Phil   A long time.

Jack   Since we were midgets, Phil. Now, all right, we have our differences, our points of *view*, but basically –

Phil   Yeah.

Jack   Basically we're friends, you and me, friends, yes?

Phil   We're friends.

Jack   That's right we are, and we're not gonna forget that 'cause of a little – I'm not. I swear *I'm* not. I know what's right, Phil, I do, and I know what's wrong, and . . . so . . . so . . . don't be mad at me, okay?

Phil I'm not mad at you.

Jack You're not? I knew it, Phil, you big hunk, I love you. (*He hugs* **Phil**. *Pause.*) So . . . can I have the apartment? (**Phil** *looks at him. Pause. He turns to go.*) Phil . . . (**Phil** *starts off.*) Hey, Phil . . . Phil! What is that supposed to be, an answer? I'm *talking* to you, Phil! (**Phil** *keeps walking.*) Oh yeah? Then *fuck* you. I will *make* my arrangements. And you know *nothing*. Live with *that*. (**Phil** *exits.*) You fucking . . . child. (*Pause. He sits. Silence.* **Carla** *enters in evening dress. She stands next to* **Jack**.)

Carla Howdy stranger.

Jack Hi.

Carla Guess what.

Jack What.

Carla I'm having a *good* time. How about you? (**Jack** *nods.*) Ah, the silent type. I like that in a fella. Wanna get married?

Jack Sure. (*She sits.*)

Carla I'm a little drunk.

Jack No.

Carla Yeah. I'm just gonna close my eyes a sec.

Jack You do that.

Carla I will. (*She leans her head on his shoulder.*) Did I tell you how nice you look?

Jack No.

Carla Well, I'm going to. You look very nice. I was watching you sit here saying how nice he can look. Why does he look so nice. (*She smiles to herself. Pause.*)

Jack We should get going.

Carla Mmmm.

Jack The sitter's waiting.

Carla   Home home. Home with you. Know what I'm thinking?

Jack   Uh-uh.

Carla   You're not the worst man in the world.

Jack   I'm not, huh?

Carla   No you're not. I'm afraid you're just not. (*Pause.*) But you'd like to be . . . (*She rests against his shoulder with her eyes closed.* **Jack** *looks out front. Fade out.*)

SEARCH AND DESTROY

Search and Destroy was commissioned and originally produced by South Coast Repertory (David Emmes, Producing Artistic Director; Martin Benson, Artistic Director), in Costa Mesa, California, on 12 January 1990. The cast was as follows:

Martin Mirkheim	Mark Harelik
Accountant, Dr Waxling, Carling	Jarion Monroe
Lauren, Jackie, Voice of Flight Attendant, Radio Announcer	Anni Long
Robert, Ron	Anthony Forkush
Kim	Philip Anglim
Marie, Terry	Dendrie Taylor
Roger, State Trooper	Hubert Baron Kelly
Hotel Clerk, Lee	Dom Magwili
Security Guard, Nuñez	Art Koustik
Bus Driver, Pamfilo	Vic Trevino

Directed by David Chambers
Designed by Chris Barreca
Costumes by Dunya Ramicova
Lighting by Chris Parry
Sound by David Budries

Search and Destroy was subsequently presented by the Yale Repertory Theatre (Stan Wojewodski, Artistic Director), in New Haven, Connecticut, on 27 November 1990. The production team was the same. The cast was as follows:

Martin Mirkheim	Joe Urla
Accountant, Dr Waxling	Jarion Monroe
Lauren	Claudia Feldstein
Robert, Ron	Anthony Forkush
Jackie, Terry, Radio Announcer	Amy Povich
Kim	Keith Szarabajka
Marie	Welker White
Roger	Jeffrey Wright

Hotel Clerk, **Carling**	William Francis McGuire
Security Guard	Christopher Bauer
Bus Driver, **State Trooper**	Robert Beatty, Jr
Nuñez	Michael Manuel
Pamfilo	Jose Zuniga
Lee	Thom Sesma

Search and Destroy was originally produced on Broadway by the Circle in the Square Theatre (Ted Mann, Artistic Director), in New York City, on 26 February 1992.

Martin Mirkheim	Griffin Dunne
Accountant	James Noah
Lauren, **Jackie**, **Radio Announcer**	Jane Fleiss
Robert	T. G. Waites
Kim	Keith Szarabajka
Marie, **Terry**	Welker White
Roger	Gregory Simmons
Hotel Clerk, **Carling**	Michael Hammond
Security Guard, **Nuñez**	Jerry Grayson
Dr Waxling	Stephen McHattie
Bus Driver, **State Trooper**	Mike Hodge
Ron	Paul Guilfoyle
Pamfilo	Arnold Molina
Lee	Thom Sesma

Directed by David Chambers
Designed by Chris Barreca
Costumes by Candice Donnelly
Lighting by Chris Parry
Sound by David Budries

Originally produced on Broadway by Circle in the Square. Commissioned and originally produced by South Coast Repertory.
Further developed by Yale Repertory Theatre.

Search and Destroy received its British premiere at the Royal Court Theatre, London, on 4 May 1993. The cast was as follows:

Martin Mirkheim	David Bamber
Accountant, Security Guard, Lee	Cyril Nri
Lauren, Jackie, Terry	Adrienne Thomas
Robert, Hotel Clerk,	
Bus Driver, Ron	Danny Webb
Kim	Andrew Woodall
Marie, Radio Announcer	Cathryn Bradshaw
Roger, Pamfilo, State Trooper	Leo Wringer
Dr Waxling, Nuñez, Carling	Colin Stinton

Directed by Stephen Daldry
Costumes by Jennifer Cook
Lighting by Johanna Town
Sound by Paul Arditti

Characters

Martin Mirkheim	**Dr Waxling**
Accountant	**Bus Driver**
Lauren	**Ron**
Robert	**Pamfilo**
Jackie	**Nuñez**
Kim	**Lee**
Marie	**Terry**
Roger	**State Trooper**
Hotel Clerk	**Radio Announcer**
Security Guard	**Carling**

Time
The present.

Place
The United States of America.

As the house lights dim.

Man's Voice (*over speakers*)   I get letters. Yes I do. People with problems. 'Dr Waxling, I see you on television . . . Dr Waxling I am *confused*, Dr Waxling I'm in *trouble*, I turn to *you* . . . as a last resort.' To me. A message for these viewers. I hope they're watching. I'm only saying it once. 'I'm trapped by my limitations,' there *are* no limitations, ANYTHING IS POSSIBLE. 'I can't escape the past,' the past is *dead*, THROW IT AWAY. 'I'm *worried*. I don't feel *safe*. I *want* to change but I'm *frightened* by my OWN WEAKNESS.' Is that *you*? Is that your 'problem'? Then I tell you *what*. You better be strong. It's that simple. *You . . . better . . . be . . . strong.*

Act One

Scene One

An office. **Martin** *in a chair,* **Accountant** *seated behind desk.*

Martin   Okay. This . . . (*Pause.*) Here is my plan. I see myself as, uh, I feel, I think my *abilities* . . . I hate fear. Hate it. Fear that makes you . . . that *stops* you. From realizing your . . . yourself. *Your . . . self.* What you *are*. What you know you could *be*. Because of that fear? No. (*Pause.* **Accountant** *shifts his papers.*) And this is not, 'Hey, make me King,' or, um, 'Why can't *I* sleep with cover girls,' because people who, that's not an *ambition*. That's . . . they don't *know* anything. The world, themselves . . . they waste their energies. On . . . what? It's foolish. Have a purpose. A *serious* purpose. Because . . . okay. Here we are, Planet Earth, boom. What's important? A neat desk? 'He was kind to children?' No. 'I will *die* one day so let me leave something behind.' Something *good*. Something *lasting*. Something of myself. Let them know I was here. Let them *know* I was here. Let them know. (*He looks at the* **Accountant***. Pause.*)

Accountant   You owe the state of Florida forty-seven thousand nine hundred and fifty-six dollars.

Martin   Uh-huh. Okay.

Accountant   Exclusive of interest and penalties.

Martin   I understand *your* position –

Accountant   You failed to file or substantially underpaid corporate taxes for the last fiscal quarter of 1990, the first fiscal quarter of 1991, the second fiscal quarter of 1991, and the fourth fiscal quarter of 1991. That is as Mirkheim Enterprises, Incorporated, doing business variously as Startime Booking, Big Top Tours, and The Southern Skating Spectacular. You are listed as sole proprietor of Mirkheim Enterprises, is that correct?

Martin   I'm trying to explain, my intentions –

Accountant   I need to know if that's correct, Mr Mirkheim. (*Pause.*)

Martin   Yes.

Accountant   In the last quarter you filed, you claimed –

Martin   My corporation –

Accountant   *Corporation* claimed as operating expenses the mortgage and maintenance on a condominium apartment in Boca Raton. This apartment is also listed as your place of residence.

Martin   Okay, *first*, I work at home so –

Accountant   You claim payment of twenty-two thousand dollars to a Ms Lauren Mirkheim as a non-exclusive consultant to your firm. We are interested in the nature of her services.

Martin   She happens to hold a business degree from –

Accountant   We are interested in seeing your records. We are interested in your *corporation's* income during the last year. We are very interested in determining –

Martin What's your point. (*Pause.*) Please.

Accountant You owe the state of Florida forty-seven thousand nine hundred fifty-six dollars. Exclusive of interest and penalties. (*Pause.*)

Martin What if I don't have it?

Accountant The state of Florida is legally empowered to place a lien upon your holdings, both real and intangible, and initiate criminal proceedings. We do not like to be taken advantage of, Mr Mirkheim.

Martin I was not taking advantage, sir, I –

Accountant How would you describe it? (*Pause.*)

Martin It's outside my main focus.

Accountant Your *main* focus.

Martin The area of my concern.

Accountant Which is.

Martin I've been *telling* you.

Accountant You're frightened of dying, was that it?

Martin No, please *listen*. I *know* how this looks. I *know* why I'm here.

Accountant Why are you here.

Martin I am here . . . because I haven't paid as much attention recently to –

Accountant That's not exactly –

Martin Attention as I should have to something you seem to . . . something important. It's important. I've let it go too long, that's a bad mistake. Now whatever my debts are I'll honour them. I give you my word. All I ask, simple request, not to be bullied, not to be threatened. I'm speaking to you openly because I believe there's a better way to be. So when I say I'm trying to achieve something, and haven't had time to attend to every –

Accountant   You're a young man, Mr Mirkheim.

Martin   Can I just –

Accountant   You're a very young man with a healthy income and a bad attitude towards reporting it. I suggest you *make* time for matters of more pressing import.

Martin   Such as?

Accountant   Forty-seven thousand nine hundred –

Martin   No, now you're – Is that supposed to *scare* me? I owe *money*? Some *numbers*? You think that's what *counts*?

Accountant   It might warrant *my* respect.

Martin   I bet it would.

Accountant   Excuse me?

Martin   You'd be down on your knees shaking. You'd be sobbing to Jesus. (*Pause.*)

Accountant   You owe us, Mr Mirkheim. It's time to pay. This office will be in touch with you shortly. You might find the services of a lawyer useful.

Martin   I don't need one.

Accountant   Your expertise is vast.

Martin   Are we done?

Accountant   For now.

Martin   Let me tell you something.

Accountant   Mmm-hmm.

Martin   This country . . . (*The* **Accountant** *looks away.*) Excuse me . . . (*The* **Accountant** *looks at him.*)

Accountant   Yes?

Martin   . . . Is about *possibilities*.

Accountant   I'll keep that in mind, Mr Mirkheim. Have a nice day.

Scene Two

A sun deck. **Lauren** *on chaise longue in bathing suit,* **Martin,** *in suit and tie, on top of her.*

Lauren   (*after a moment*)   Marty. (*Pause.*) Marty.

Martin   Yes.

Lauren   Please.

Martin   What.

Lauren   Don't fuck me on the sun deck. (*Pause.*)

Martin   Why not?

Lauren   I don't *want* you to. (*Pause.*)

Martin   Let's go inside.

Lauren   No.

Martin   Come on.

Lauren   The cleaning lady's there.

Martin   She won't see us.

Lauren   Marty. *Marty.* (*Pause.*) We're not doing any more of this. It's *over.* Okay? (*Pause.* **Martin** *stands up.*) I thought you were trying celibacy.

Martin   I am.

Lauren   You should try harder.

Martin   I should. I'm going to. I *will.* (*Pause. He picks up a book lying by the chaise.*) Still on the same chapter.

Lauren   It's a long book.

Martin   He says some very important things in here.

Lauren   Well.

Martin   About the world. How to live.

Lauren   Since when do you read?

Martin   Since now.

Lauren . I just can't get into it.

Martin   He's on TV every week. You could watch with me.

Lauren   Let's not start.

Martin   We could be together.

Lauren   Marty, make up your mind.

Martin   I *want* us together. I wanted us to *change* together.

Lauren   I'm happy the way I am.

Martin   Everyone says that.

Lauren   I know it. I know how *I* feel.

Martin   You shouldn't do coke.

Lauren   Well thank God I never saw you trying to suck your face off a mirror.

Martin   I'm done with all that.

Lauren   I forgot, you're a new man.

Martin   I'm trying to be.

Lauren   We're not kids now, Marty.

Martin   That's exactly *why*.

Lauren   So walk out on me, give up a good business –

Martin   No, no, I didn't 'give it up', I –

Lauren   Running around the country five years, finally I think I get to stay in one --

Martin   Lauren, Lauren, *listen* to me, the business was nothing. Circus tours. Booking wrestlers. Polka bands. It proved nothing. What is *that*. What have I *done*.

Lauren What've you done, you have a condo, you have –

Martin No. Not things. Deeds. I'm talking about deeds. (*Pause.*)

Lauren My lawyer thinks you shouldn't be here.

Martin I'm going.

Lauren I'm sorry I have to say that.

Martin I have an appointment anyway.

Lauren And you'll take care of that cheque.

Martin Yeah, I, just forgot to transfer the money. It'll clear this time. (*Pause.*) Can you wait a week, ten days?

Lauren Again?

Martin Last time. I promise. There's a project I'm working on. Something I care about. When it's done everything'll be different.

Lauren Will it.

Martin Yes. I wish you could understand that. (*Pause.*)

Lauren All right.

Martin Thank you. (*He offers her the book.*) Here.

Lauren It's okay.

Martin I can get another copy.

Lauren I'm done with the book, Marty. (*Pause.*) What is it?

Martin Hmm?

Lauren What's your project? (**Martin** *looks out front. Pause.*)

Martin You can see clear to the horizon from here.

Scene Three

A terrace. Evening. **Martin** *in his suit.* **Robert** *in casual wear. Sounds of a party from inside.*

Robert   Where'd it go, Marty.

Martin   I don't know, Rob.

Robert   Where'd all that money *go*, you know. I mean Jesus. Six hundred points they're saying 'no cause for alarm'. *Fuck* me. (*Pause.*)

Martin   How much did you lose?

Robert   A lot. Boodles. Great entire boodles. Fuck fuck why didn't I see this coming. Why am I throwing this *party*.

Martin   You'll make it back.

Robert   Will I. (*Pause.*) How'd you come out.

Martin   I'm not too worried.

Robert   You're not.

Martin   It's just, you know, the economy.

Robert   Just that, huh?

Martin   Yeah.

Robert   God bless you, Marty. (**Jackie**, **Robert**'s *wife, enters. She sees* **Martin**.)

Jackie   Oh. (*To* **Robert**.) Are you spending the whole evening out here?

Robert   I'd like to enjoy my terrace before I jump off it.

Jackie   It's your friends in there, not mine.

Robert   Honey, I kinda lost several hundred thousand dollars today. Be nice to me.

Martin   Hello, Jackie.

Jackie   Yes. (*She exits. Pause.*)

Martin   She's mad at me.

Robert   Well, you know, Lauren's calling her.

Martin   Yah.

Robert   What do you want, they're sisters. (*Pause.*) Tell you what my broker says.

Martin   What.

Robert   Fear.

Martin   What about it?

Robert   He thinks it's going to be big. He thinks we're gonna be hearing a lot from fear in the nineties. It's going to be the fear *decade*. And he says . . . (*A man,* **Kim,** *walks onto the terrace.* **Robert** *drops his voice.*) He says now's the time to ground-floor it.

Martin   Fear?

Robert   Fear-related industries. Blood analysers. Viral filters. UV screens. Toteable security systems. Impact-proof leisure wear, I've seen that. I mean this is you walk into K-Mart, you go buy something make you feel safe. Very cutting edge, very hot. Which sounds great except here I am stuck with my pants around my ankles three hundred k in the hole. Majorly sucks. (*Pause. Party noise from inside.*)

Martin (*producing book*)   You read this, Rob?

Robert (*not looking at it*)   Wish I had time, Marty.

Martin   You should.

Robert   What's it, the Trump thing? Dead meat, kid, dead meat.

Martin   No, he talks about all this stuff. And what it *means.*

Robert   Who does.

Martin   Doctor Waxling.

Robert   I'm sorry?

Martin   Luther Waxling. Who wrote the book. (*Pause.*)

Robert   Guy on cable three in the morning?

Martin   Yes.

Robert   Staying up late, buddy boy. (*He looks at the book.*) *Daniel Strong.*

Martin   Right.

Robert   Looks interesting.

Martin   No, you're only saying, but it is.

Robert   I'm sure.

Martin   He, what he does, it's the story of this young, Daniel, Strong, it starts, he's born –

Robert   Uh-huh.

Martin   And he grows up in this, the world, where the system, the schools and everything, it, it *crushes* him, inside, they teach him to be worthless –

Robert   Yeah, right.

Martin   And then, as a man, he goes on a jour – an *adventure*, which, he discovers within *himself* the power -- (**Jackie** *enters.*)

Jackie   Your business partner's doing lines in the playroom.

Robert   Shit.

Jackie   We agreed no drugs tonight.

Robert   He was clean at the door.

Jackie   Well he scored off somebody.

Robert   Yeah, I'll, okay. (**Jackie** *exits.*) Marty, excuse me.

Martin   I just want to tell you about this.

Robert   Sounds great, really –

Martin   Yeah, so, I want to *do* something with it.

Robert   Huh?

Martin   I want to buy the book, the rights to the book, and do something with it.

Robert   You want to . . .

Martin   Buy the rights. Make a movie. (*Pause.* **Robert** *laughs.*) What's funny?

Robert   'Mirkheim Studios Presents . . .'

Martin   So? (**Robert** *keeps laughing.*) Why not?

Robert   No, good luck.

Martin   You think I can't do it?

Robert   I . . . It's not like booking Smurfs On Ice, Mart.

Martin   I'm aware of that.

Robert   You see good money, Mart. What do you want, respect?

Martin   I want to *achieve* something –

Robert   Bad time for that, boyo. Trust me. *Good* time for sticking to what you know and holding on to what you got, yes?

Martin   No, 'cause by applying my *abilities* –

Robert   Mart. Honestly. Honestly now. Let's not . . . *overestimate*, huh? Who we are?

Martin   What are you saying?

Robert   I'm saying . . . what am I saying, you been lucky. It was easy pickings these last few years and we've *all* been very lucky. But top of the food chain you're not. (*Pause.*) And I *speak* this out of love.

Martin   I thought you could help me.

Robert   What I'm doing.

Martin   Not like this.

Robert   You want money? I can't *give* you money. I set you up once, I can't do that now.

Martin   I don't want money. I want contacts. You know people.

Robert   I know *some* people.

Martin   So put me in touch with them. (*Pause.*)

Robert   Did you *talk* to the guy?

Martin   Which.

Robert   The book guy.

Martin   Not yet.

Robert   So if you can buy the thing you don't even know. (*Pause.*) Marty? Right?

Martin   It's not a problem.

Robert   Why's that.

Martin   Because when I meet him he'll see.

Robert   What, that you floss nightly?

Martin   That I understand what he's talking about. We have to change, Rob. Can't you feel that? We all have to *change*. (**Robert** *looks at him. Pause.* **Jackie** *enters and stands there.*)

Robert   *Okay.* (*He turns and starts off with her. To* **Martin**:) Call me later.

Martin   Does that mean you'll help?

Robert   It means call me later. (*They exit.* **Martin** *looks out. Silence.*)

Kim   People waste their time.

Martin   Pardon?

Kim   They waste their time. They make excuses, they consider the fine points, they start arguments. Factors arise. Moments pass. Directions are mislaid. We sit in the car.

We wonder where we were going, and why we had to get there. You smoke?

Martin   No.

Kim   I do. Helps me think. You mind? (**Martin** *shakes his head.* **Kim** *lights a cigarette.*) Get evenings like this in the Mediterranean.

Martin   Do you.

Kim   Oh yes. (*Pause.*)

Martin (*offering his hand*)   Martin Mirkheim.

Kim   Kim Feston.

Martin   You're not a friend of Rob's?

Kim   No.

Martin   I didn't think so. (*Pause.*)

Kim   And are you in business, Martin?

Martin   Well, I . . . yes.

Kim   I say this: God bless the businessmen.

Martin   Why's that.

Kim   They are the . . . *agents* of our hope.

Martin   Huh. (*Pause.*) That's a lovely phrase.

Kim   You appreciate language.

Martin   I'm not good at it myself . . .

Kim   But you're keen to the possibilities.

Martin   It just strikes me a certain way.

Kim   You are not a modern man. (*Pause.*)

Martin   And yourself?

Kim   Yes?

Martin   Are you in business?

Kim   On occasion.

Martin   Ah.

Kim   In a freelance capacity. With an overseas consultancy firm. Mostly based in New York.

Martin   What brings you here?

Kim   Doing some work. For your friend's partner I *think*.

Martin   Sounds interesting.

Kim   Well. (*Pause. They look at each other.*) I've read that, you know.

Martin   *Daniel Strong?*

Kim   Uh-huh.

Martin   You're kidding.

Kim   No. It had a . . . powerful effect on me.

Martin   Really.

Kim   Oh yes. That scene on the mountain-top.

Martin   Hmm, he's all alone, he's lost, starving . . .

Kim   The sun begins to rise, the city stretched out far below . . .

Martin   He remembers the day he killed his father.

Kim   He hears a voice –

Martin   His *own* voice saying what?

Kim   'There was nothing to be forgiven. And anything was possible.'

Martin   Right. Right.

Kim   The best book when you're nineteen. (*Pause.*)

Martin   I'm going to make a movie of it.

Kim   Yes. I overheard. What a superb idea.

Martin   You're not in the . . . film –

Kim No.

Martin Sorry.

Kim Oh, don't apologize. We don't have to do that. (*He smiles.* **Robert** *enters with* **Jackie** *behind him. Pause.*)

Robert Uh . . . yeah. Um . . . (*Pause.*) Look. I'm really sorry about this. I'm gonna . . . I'm afraid gonna have to ask you to, ah, to leave my house. I'm sorry. (*Pause.*)

Kim Are you speaking to me?

Robert Yah. (*Pause.*)

Kim Why?

Jackie You know why. (**Kim** *and* **Jackie** *look at each other. Pause.*)

Kim Thank you for having me. You spread a lovely buffet.

Jackie You're welcome.

Kim (*to* **Martin**) We should talk more. If you're ever in New York . . . give me a call. I mean that. (*He hands* **Martin** *a business card and exits.* **Martin** *watches him go, then turns to* **Robert** *and* **Jackie**.)

Martin What . . . (**Robert** *gestures 'don't ask' and starts walking away.* **Martin** *stops him.*) Rob. I'll do it myself.

Robert Huh?

Martin I'm going to do it myself. (**Robert** *looks at him. Pause.*)

Robert This fucking *day* . . .

Scene Four

Another office. A receptionist, **Marie**, *behind desk.* **Martin** *stands before her with a small bandage on his temple.*

Martin I'd like to see Dr Waxling.

Marie   Is he expecting you?

Martin   Oh yes.

Marie   Your name, please?

Martin   Martin Mirkheim.

Marie   Thank you. (*She picks up phone.*) Mr Mirkheim to see Dr Waxling. (*Pause.*) He says so, yes. (*Pause. To* **Martin**.) May I ask what this is in reference to?

Martin   It's a personal matter.

Marie (*into phone*)   He's says it's personal. (*Pause. To* **Martin**.) He'll be right with you.

Martin   He will. Thank you. (*Pause.*) Is the show taped here in Dallas?

Marie   Huh?

Martin   Dr Waxling's show, taped in the building?

Marie   No. The station.

Martin   Of course.

Marie   These are the Waxling Institute's International Headquarters.

Martin   Ah. (*Silence.* **Roger** *enters in business suit.*)

Roger   Hello.

Martin   Hi.

Roger   I'm Roger.

Martin   Yes. All right.

Roger   You wanted to see Dr Waxling.

Martin   Correct.

Roger   That's not possible right now.

Martin   Why?

Roger   He's busy.

Martin   I see.

Roger   Perhaps I can help you.

Martin   It's a personal matter.

Roger   Of what nature?

Martin   A personal nature. (*Pause.*)

Roger   Well, we're very happy you've walked in, sir. Getting personal is what we're about.

Martin   Thank you.

Roger   You should know that Dr Waxling requests applicants first complete the Mastery Sessions before individual consultation. A lot of what he says is based on exposure to the introductory material. Now I'd be happy to set up an appointment with one of our –

Martin   Who are you?

Roger   Excuse me?

Martin   Who *are* you?

Roger   I'm Roger. I'm Dr Waxling's assistant.

Martin   Roger. Okay. I'm not here for that. Would you please tell him that Martin Mirkheim wants to see him. I am president of Mirkheim Enterprises, Incorporated. I have flown here directly from Florida and I have something very important to discuss with him.

Roger   What would that company be, sir?

Martin   Mirkheim Enterprises is a diversified organization focused primarily in the field of entertainment.

Roger   I'm not familiar with it.

Martin   We're a prominent presence in the south-eastern states.

Roger   Ah.

Martin   I own, my company owns, several television

stations in Florida and, *Georgia*, WKRG there, we also have interests, are *active in*, the, area, of motion picture production, which, maybe you've heard, it's primed for very very explosive growth on the Peninsula with heavy involvement from the major studios.

Roger   I wasn't aware of that.

Martin   Yes, very exciting. We're about to enter into an agreement with Twentieth Cent – legally I shouldn't say, and ah, unfortunately I have a busy schedule in Dallas, leaving tomorrow, I'm meeting very shortly with some petroleum people, if Doctor Waxling wishes to talk I'm afraid it's going to have to be in the next half-hour. (*Pause.*)

Roger   And that would be in reference to . . .

Martin   The matter I've mentioned.

Roger   The personal matter.

Martin   Yes. (*Pause.*)

Roger   I'm sorry sir, you're out of luck. Doctor Waxling is taping all day.

Martin   Ah, Roger. Yes. That's very good. I realize you're just doing your job, but –

Roger   Sir, I've told you –

Martin   I don't think you quite understand what –

Roger   No. No, I do understand, sir. I do. You want to see the Doctor. You can't. I will certainly tell him you stopped *in* . . . and I hope you enjoy your stay in Dallas.

Martin   Listen, your behaviour –

Roger   Mr Mirkheim. This building has an excellent security staff.

Martin   It does.

Roger   Yes. (*Pause.*) Goodbye. (*He shakes* **Martin***'s hand and exits. Pause.* **Martin** *rises and turns to* **Marie**.)

Martin   How come no one here has an accent?

Marie   You mean like a Texas accent?

Martin   Yah.

Marie   Well, you know. Everybody's from everywhere.

Martin   Hum. (*Pause.*) Was he someone important?

Marie   He thinks so. (*Pause.*) You're a producer?

Martin   Pardon?

Marie   A movie producer?

Martin   Yes. That *is* what I am.

Marie   Huh, what kind movies?

Martin   Various . . . kinds.

Marie   Like slasher stuff?

Martin   No.

Marie   People talking ones.

Martin   I suppose.

Marie   Those are okay.

Martin   Well.

Marie   Anything I would know? (*Pause.*)

Martin   Did you see *Field of Dreams*?

Marie   Yuh.

Martin   I was involved on that.

Marie   Huh. (*Pause.*) Bang your head?

Martin   Sorry?

Marie   Your head.

Martin   Oh. No. (*Pause.*) Well. (*He starts out.*)

Marie   Could I send you one?

Martin   Send me what?

Marie   One I wrote. A script.

Martin   Ah.

Marie   Yeah, I took a class, I mean, why not, right? 'Cause I *have* ideas.

Martin   Right.

Marie   Could, would you mind if I did? (*Pause.*)

Martin   What's your name?

Marie   Marie.

Martin   Marie. Hi. Listen –

Marie   I know, send it to your whatever.

Martin   No. No, I don't work that way, Marie. I don't treat people like that. I would like to hear about your script.

Marie   Really.

Martin   I *can't* right now.

Marie   Sure, thanks.

Martin   I'm leaving tomorrow. I could – no, I'm sorry.

Marie   What?

Martin   No, it wouldn't sound right. Send me your script.

Marie   What wouldn't?

Martin   I'm free tonight, but to –

Marie   You want me to come to your hotel. (*Pause.*) Right?

Martin   *My* hotel. Ah. (*Pause.*) Yah, sure. Why don't you do that. I'm at the Omni Atrium. It's over by –

Marie   It's right by the airport.

Martin   Yes. Exactly.

Marie   There's a restaurant there. If you want to eat.

Martin   The hotel? Of course. I hope you'll be my guest.

Marie   I mean in the airport. (*Pause.*)

Martin   Well, that's fine too.

Marie   Okay. (*Pause.*) I know something you don't.

Martin   What?

Marie   There's blood on you.

Martin   Where? (*She points at his tie.* **Martin** *lifts it up to reveal a half-dollar sized spot of blood.* **Marie** *touches it with her finger.*) It's still wet. (*She holds up her finger.* **Martin** *looks at it. The phone rings twice.*)

Scene Five

An airport snack bar. **Martin** *holding bound script,* **Marie**.

Marie   Everybody's dead all over. Okay. She's caught. The spinesucker has her pinned against the wall. With his other hand he cracks open her boyfriend's head and smears his brains all over her tits. Okay. The elevator's stuck between floors. This thing comes out of him like a gangrene penis with a lobster claw and starts burrowing into her. The pain's unbearable. Okay. Finally she manages to reach the switch on the radial saw and rips it into him. But he just smiles, okay, his stomach opens up and he absorbs it, like he does and goes on pumping her up. She's gonna die, that's all. *Except* inside him the saw's still going, spinning around, he starts shaking and there's a, what do you, close shot, yeah, and the saw rips out of his chest, there's this explosion of meat and pus pouring out like from a fire hose, he climbs on her and tries to shove the penis claw down her throat, okay, but she hacks it off with the saw okay he goes shooting back against the glass doors okay they break he falls five floors, onto the metal spike in the fountain it goes straight through his face, his brains spurt out and slide into the water like fresh cum okay. He's dead, he's dead, he's finally fucking dead. She walks away that's the end. (*Pause.*)

Martin   And this is your *first* script.

Marie   No. I wrote one in class.

Martin   Ah. (*Pause.*) The same sort of – ?

Marie   Horror, yeah, I like the horror.

Martin   Mmm.

Marie   Makes you feel something.

Martin   Yes. (*Pause.*) It's very violent.

Marie   You wouldn't do that?

Martin   I might.

Marie   How much would you pay me for it?

Martin   That depends.

Marie   Half a million dollars?

Martin   I have to read it first.

Marie   Sure. (*Pause.*)

Martin   How's the burger?

Marie   Okay.

Martin   They just leave them sitting under heat lamps all day.

Marie   I don't come here for the food. (*Pause.*)

Martin   You from Dallas, Marie?

Marie   Cincinnati.

Martin   What's that like?

Marie   This. Basically like this.

Martin   How long you been working for the Doctor.

Marie   Few months.

Martin   Have much to do with him?

Marie   Sometimes. Sometimes much.

Martin   Tough man to get to.

Marie   You shoulda made an appointment first.

Martin   There was a little mix-up.

Marie   I would of let you in, but Roger . . .

Martin   He seems very dedicated.

Marie   Two tabs Dexadrine he thinks he's Mighty Mouse. You told him you know the Doctor?

Martin   Well, I don't like to throw names around. We'll get it all straightened out tomorrow.

Marie   You're seeing the Doctor tomorrow?

Martin   I do have other business, but possibly I could squeeze –

Marie   'Cause I think he's starting a lecture tour tomorrow.

Martin   What?

Marie   Yeah, he's gonna be in Minneapolis.

Martin   Minneapolis.

Marie   Right. In Minnesota. (*Pause.*) Are you all right?

Martin   Oh yes. I'm fine. He told me, of course. I forgot. Minneapolis.

Marie   Big trip for nothing, huh.

Martin   For nothing, no, I met you, I have, there's your *script*, ah, *Dead World* . . .

Marie   My teacher says it's not a good title.

Martin   Oh no, very eye-catching.

Marie   Thanks. (*Silence. Jet takes off.* **Marie** *follows it with her eyes. Pause.*) That's the last plane for two hours.

Martin   They'll probably want to close up.

Marie   You can sit here all night, they don't care.

Martin   Is that what you're going to do?

Marie   I don't know.

Martin   Well, I better get back. I'm up early tomorrow, some big meetings in town before I fly out.

Marie   Okay. (*Pause.*) Kye ask you a question?

Martin   Of course.

Marie   How come you lie so much?

Martin   What?

Marie   You lie a lot. (*Pause.*)

Martin   How do you mean?

Marie   Um ... the office this afternoon you lied you had an appointment, you said some stuff to Roger I don't know sounded kinda stupid you told me the Doctor knows you maybe he does I don't think so. And the other stuff about the movies and everything, I kinda wonder about, 'cause the movies, that's California, you're in Dallas, you're sitting in the airport snack bar and you're talking to *me*. And I'm not anybody.

Martin   Uh-huh.

Marie   So that's a lot of lying in the time I know you, which isn't very long. (*Pause.*)

Martin   Does that bother you?

Marie   It might. I lie. I don't do it right. I lie at the end when I'm scared and I don't get anything. You're lying at the beginning. What do you want to get? (*Pause.*)

Martin   Marie.

Marie   Yah.

Martin   I need your help.

Marie   What for?

Martin   I *have* to get to Doctor Waxling. I flew here from Florida. I'll fly to Minneapolis, I don't care. I have to reach him.

Marie   Why?

Martin   Because . . . all right. Yes. I lied, I lied, I did. I'm a liar. I don't want to be. I *want* to be true. To make myself *become* true. But it's so hard, Marie. You know what I'm saying?

Marie   You're not a movie producer.

Martin   That's not the point –

Marie   Are you?

Martin   No I'm not. Yes I *am*. I *am* a producer. No, I *haven't* made a movie. So what. So *what*, right? I am what I say I am because what . . . what you say you *are*, that's what you'll be.

Marie   Just by saying it.

Martin   Okay. Okay. I understand. You're thinking, what is he, he lures me here, no, lures me, he's promising things, my script, get me into *bed* . . . all right. I *admit* it. There it is. But . . . but . . . listen to me. Do you believe in anything?

Marie   Do I . . .

Martin   Believe in anything. (*Pause.*)

Marie   Not especially.

Martin   I do. Now this is true. I *do* believe. I believe in myself. I believe in my power to affect things. And if you help me, you will have that power too. I need to meet the Doctor. I *need* to get his book. The rights to his book *Daniel Strong*. That means something to me. It *means* something. I know you feel that. I know you *understand* what I'm saying. I know it. (*Pause.*)

Marie If you went to Minneapolis . . .

Martin I will do that. Yes. Then what?

Marie What I could do is get you a pass. For backstage. You just walk through.

Martin And then I would . . .

Marie Talk to him.

Martin The Doctor.

Marie Yeah.

Martin Can I mention your name?

Marie Um . . .

Martin Or is not a good idea.

Marie Not a good idea.

Martin I completely understand. (*Pause.*) Marie.

Marie I know, you're welcome.

Martin No, that's not what I was going to say. I . . .
(*Pause.*)

Marie Yeah?

Martin I want to tell you that I feel very . . . *connected* to you right now. And in this world . . . at this *time* . . . that matters.

Marie Thank you. (*Pause. She takes his hand, rests it on the table, and spreads the fingers.*) You seem tense.

Martin I am. I'm tense. (*Pause.*) My plane . . .

Marie   Sorry?

Martin   I, my plane today, it's, we had a non-standard touchdown.

Marie   A crash?

Martin   No. Not a crash. It's not called a crash. Landing gear wouldn't open. They had to spray the runway with foam so we could slide in. (*Pause.*)

Marie   Did anyone die?

Martin   No. Actually. I cut my forehead.

Marie   Were you afraid?

Martin   I tried not to be. I tried to *make* myself not . . . I couldn't. Um. Couldn't get away from it. That fear. Of . . . yeah. (*Pause.*) At this moment I'm finding myself very attracted to you.

Marie   Uh-huh.

Martin   I've taken a vow of *celibacy* . . .

Marie   You have.

Martin   I just wanted to tell you that.

Marie   Okay. (*Pause.*) I'm gonna tell *you* a secret, Mr Mirkheim. That nobody knows.

Martin   Yes.

Marie   Why this place is good.

Martin   Why.

Marie   Be quiet. Be very quiet inside yourself. Don't think. Don't look at me. What do you hear. (*Pause.*)

Martin   Nothing. I . . . (*Pause.*) Nothing.

Marie   That's right. (*She puts his hand against her forehead.*) If you close your eyes? You can feel the strip lights humming. (*She closes her eyes.* **Martin** *looks at her. Faint humming sound.*)

Scene Six

Hotel desk. **Martin**, **Clerk**.

Clerk   Did you enjoy your stay at the Omni Atrium, sir?

Martin   Oh yes indeed.

Clerk   Make sure the bill is right, that was the Cattleman Suite one night, three twenty-eight sixty-five for a double . . .

Martin   Single.

Clerk   Pardon?

Martin   Single. Just me.

Clerk   Oh. I see. (*Pause.*) I understood you had a guest.

Martin   A guest.

Clerk   In the suite. Staying. (*Pause.*)

Martin   Right. Very good. Just, ah, put it on the card.

Clerk   Yes sir.

Martin   She –

Clerk   I understand completely. (*He puts card through phone link.*)

Martin   Great. (*Pause.*) So they watch that lobby, huh.

Clerk   Well, our security's pretty state of the art. We don't want the guests to have any cause for alarm or – (*Loud beep.*) Okay. Ah. We're not getting clearance here, sir.

Martin   We're not.

Clerk   Uh-uh. (*Pause.*)

Martin   What's that, the – ?

Clerk   VISA.

Martin   Right. Right, that's the *company's* – here, put it on my personal – (*He takes out another card.*) – Tell you what, make it easy, we'll do cash. Not gonna tell me you don't take cash, are you.

Clerk   Course we do, sir.

Martin *(as he counts out bills)*   Glad to hear it.

Clerk   Sorry about this.

Martin   Hey, that's your job. Take it seriously.

Clerk   I do, sir.

Martin   I see that. I think it's terrific. I really do.

Clerk   Just trying to get somewhere.

Martin   You will, believe me. This is yours. *(He holds out a twenty-dollar bill.)* No, come on. Really.

Clerk *(taking it)*   Thank you sir. Have a *very* good trip.

Martin   Oh, I'm going to. I know I'm going to. This just absolutely has to be the most incredibly fine day. (**Clerk** *turns to register.* **Martin** *looks at credit card.*)

Scene Seven

Meeting room. Overhead projector standing next to podium with 'Rodeway Inn' plaque.

Transparency on wall reading:

THE FOUR RULES OF SUCCESS

1. STRENGTH NEEDS NO EXCUSE.
2. THE PAST IS POINTLESS.
3. JUST BECAUSE IT HAPPENED TO YOU DOESN'T MAKE IT INTERESTING.
4. THE THINGS YOU APOLOGIZE FOR ARE THE THINGS YOU WANT.

Martin *handcuffed to chair. Security Guard, in suit and tie, sitting opposite. Silence.*

Martin   Indian name, isn't it?

Guard   What.

Martin   Minneapolis?

Guard   American.

Martin   One last question.

Guard   Mmm.

Martin   *Are* these necessary?

Guard   Your behaviour made them necessary.

Martin   Because you grabbed me. Sir. *You* grabbed *me*. Would you like that? Would you want that *done* to you? Sir? (*Pause.*) You're *employed* by Dr Waxling?

Guard   I'm employed to protect the security of this motel.

Martin   I had a pass.

Guard   You were asked to leave.

Martin   A *pass*, sir.

Guard   Function was ended.

Martin   My flight was late, that's not a crime.

Guard   Function ends, room's closed.

Martin   And that's a law.

Guard   It's policy.

Martin   It's policy, why are you *keeping* me here?

Guard   By request.

Martin   From whom?

Guard   Couldn't say.

Martin   Sir. (**Guard** *looks at him.*) We *make* the world. However we choose to act, that's what this world will be. Just consider it. (**Guard** *looks away. Silence.* **Roger** *enters.*)

Roger   Hello.

Martin   Hi.

Roger   Mr Mirkheim, isn't it?

Martin   Roger. Good to see you.

Roger   You like to travel, Mr Mirkheim.

Martin   Yes, I do.

Roger   How did you enjoy Dallas?

Martin   *Loved* it. Great city, great people.

Roger   Took care of your business there?

Martin   Mmm-*hmm*.

Roger   And here you are in Minneapolis.

Martin   I am indeed. (*Pause.*)

Roger   Now this pass, Mr Mirkheim.

Martin   Yes.

Roger   Obviously I'm *curious* . . . how'd you get it?

Martin   Ha.

Roger   No, but really.

Martin   I don't think that matters.

Roger   You don't.

Martin   No.

Roger   Fair enough. (*Pause.*) You're from where'd you say
Florida?

Martin   That's right.

Roger   Live in Boca Raton down there, nice town.

Martin   Oh yes.

Roger   Run a booking agency is it? Various names.
You're legally separated from your wife. You were born in
Rigdewood New Jersey. You're not in the film business.
You're not talking to any studios. You're not making deals,
huh?

Martin   Where'd you get this?

Roger   Just, basically, we can agree on these facts, right?

Martin   Who *told* you this?

Roger   These are just facts, Mr Mirkheim. Very basic facts about a person's life, very easily obtained. Now I bet there are other facts, maybe not quite so easy to find, but nonetheless worthwhile, especially when heard in a court of law.

Martin   Okay. We need to stop right here 'cause what you're doing, you're threatening me, that doesn't work.

Roger   It doesn't.

Martin   No, 'cause that's the *past*. You're talking about the past and whatever happened to whoever it was, it's not me. I'm here right now and *that's* me and what *is* at this moment, *that* is what I will deal with. Talk to me about that.

Roger   I see.

Martin   No you don't. You think I'm like you, and the things you're scared of, your reputation, your good *name* or being punished, that's worthless. I know you. I know what you do. You're still worried mommy'll find the tissues under the bed. (*Pause.* **Roger** *takes out a small memo book.*)

Roger   (*reading*)   305 673-5400.

Martin   What?

Roger   Florida Bureau of Taxation. (*Pause.*)

Martin   Yes?

Roger   I think *they* might like to hear about your recent adventures.

Martin   What'd you speak to my wife? I have to tell you my wife and I, not to cast, the thing about her, she's, a little bitter, basically she's wasting her life –

Roger   (*starting out*)   Mirkheim Enterprises, wasn't it?

Martin Okay.

Roger Excuse me?

Martin Okay. What. What. (*Pause.*)

Roger Who gave you the pass, Mr Mirkheim. (*Pause.*)

Martin The receptionist.

Roger Who is that.

Martin In Dallas. Marie.

Roger How did that happen, Mr Mirkheim.

Martin It just did.

Roger It just *came* upon her to give you this pass.

Martin That is correct.

Roger Did you know her? Before?

Martin No.

Roger But you know her now.

Martin Yes. (*Pause.*)

Roger Would you excuse me, please?

Martin Right. (**Roger** *exits. Pause. To* **Guard**:) Nice place, Minnesota?

Guard I like it.

Martin Bet you're a native, huh.

Guard I'm from Baltimore.

Martin What brought you here.

Guard Work.

Martin Good. Good for you. (**Roger** *re-enters, followed by* **Dr Waxling**.)

Roger Mr Mirkheim? This is Dr Waxling.

Martin Yes, *yes* –

Roger   He'd like to talk to you. (**Roger** *whispers briefly to* **Guard**, *who nods and exits.*)

Martin   Yes. Dr Waxling. I . . . what an honour, sir, what a *great* honour, you have been . . . I wish I could shake your hand, as you can see I'm . . . First *impressions*, huh? Let me organize my thoughts, I'm not here to bore you with my problems. The first thing I want, I *need* to tell you, is what a tremendous influence your work has – I mean drifting through my, my *life*, all the time afraid to say I don't know *anything*. I DON'T KNOW ANYTHING. Than a *baby*. And for you in your work to say 'Yes it's true and don't pretend, *yes* it's true and *that* will set you free,' has made me strong. In myself. I *believe* in myself. And for this I just would like to say . . . thank you. (*Pause.*)

Waxling   Did you fuck my woman?

Martin   Huh?

Waxling   That girl, you're fucking her?

Martin   I'm sorry, I don't . . .

Waxling   Roger.

Roger   Dr Waxling would like to know if you've had sexual congress with Marie.

Martin   No. (*Pause.*)

Waxling   Has he been frisked?

Roger   Yes sir. (**Waxling** *reaches over, grabs* **Martin** *by the lapels and slams his head against a chair.*)

Waxling   Hey. *Hey.* Do I have your attention? (**Martin** *nods.*) Two things people do really rub me the wrong way. One is *lie*, the other is fuck my women.

Martin   Not lying –

Waxling   What?

Martin   I'm not lying, sir –

Waxling   No no. No. You're fucking with my things, my

things, *mine*, I own them you don't *touch* them I don't care
who you are. I *know* that girl, she has a *low* self-image, *easily*
manipulated, don't think she won't tell me, huh?
Everything. (*Pause.*)

Martin I slept with her.

Waxling You did.

Martin Yes.

Waxling (*grabbing him again*) You greasy little fuck –

Martin That's it. Dr Waxling. That's *all*.

Waxling He *just* screwed her, that's all, guys in fucking
suits –

Martin I *slept* with her. Just, in the same bed. We slept.
(**Waxling** *holds him. Pause.*) Like Daniel Strong does. To test
himself.

Waxling Who?

Martin Daniel Strong. Daniel *Strong*. (*Pause.*)

Waxling You read that, huh. (**Martin** *nods*.) You read
my little offering. You had to come see me. Over great
distances through hardship to gaze upon my face.

Martin Yes. (*Pause.*)

Waxling Roger.

Roger Yes, Doctor.

Waxling How many.

Roger Well as I explained the print ad mix-up –

Waxling How many.

Roger Ninety-eight.

Waxling How many takers.

Roger Now some reason here a lot of Shriners –

Waxling   How many.

Roger   Two for the seminar.

Waxling   Two.

Roger   Yes. (*Pause.*)

Waxling   Where you from?

Martin   Boca Raton, it's in Flo –

Waxling   What time I'm on there.

Martin   Three a.m. Sundays.

Waxling   Oh that's fine. Really splendid. Three a.m., Rodeway Inn ninety fucking Shriners. I'm doing well. I'm making a *big* noise.

Roger   The marketing strategy –

Waxling   They're not *buying* me. I'm not being *perceived.* As a *threat.* I'm not being taken as a threat.

Roger   I think, when people get scared enough our message –

Waxling   When's *that* happening, Roger. When are they gonna get *scared?*

Roger   In *USA Today* a poll showed . . .

Waxling   Fucking TV my *room* doesn't work . . .

Roger   Homeowners' fear of – I'll have it checked –

Waxling   Get me something *chocolate.* (**Roger** *looks at* **Martin**, *then exits. Pause.*)

Martin   Very often the people who advise us –

Waxling   No. Don't.

Martin   Pardon?

Waxling   Don't try to impress me with your 'thoughts'. Please. (*Pause.*) What *is* it with you people, huh?

Martin   Who do you mean, Dr Waxling?

Waxling   I mean *you people*. Holed up in your ratty little rooms scribbling on shopping bags. 'Now my destiny seems clear . . . it will all happen today.' Not here, buddy. You're not plugging me in some hotel lobby. I'm not your double. I'm not sending messages through your schnauzer. You stay away from *me* and you stay away from my *things*. What are you, crossing guard or something? Hospital orderly?

Martin   I'm a movie producer.

Waxling   Are you now.

Martin   Yes.

Waxling   And *not* some obsessional lunatic chasing me around the country convinced I hold the key to your life.

Martin   No.

Waxling   Good. 'Cause I catch you fucking with my things again we don't mess with trespassing harassment thirty days of fun. I'll make you disappear. Produce that. (*He starts out.*)

Martin   I – Could we discuss business?

Waxling   What?

Martin   I came here to discuss business. A business proposition. For you. (*Pause.*)

Waxling   Yes?

Martin   I believe your book *Daniel Strong* has great commercial potential and I wish to offer you a substantial sum of money in exchange for the worldwide motion picture rights.

Waxling   Uh-*huh.*

Martin   Would you be interested in, in such an arrangement?

Waxling   With you?

Martin   Dr Waxling, I don't blame you for, for – This is not how I wanted to approach you. This is not according to my *plan*. Now you protect yourself. I see that and I think it's wise. Because, I hope you will allow me to say this, people aren't listening, they are twisting what you have to say, they are pushing you down. You of all people. I know how it is not to be heard. I don't want to see this happen to you. I would like to bring your message to millions of people in a simple way they can understand. And yes I would like to profit by it. I would like people to know my name. To see my name and know that I have done what they could not. That will live on when I am gone. (*Pause.* **Waxling** *takes a bottle of No-Doz and swallows three or four tablets. He looks at* **Martin**.)

Waxling   It's basically an adventure story.

Martin   And what a story.

Waxling   It has certain other . . . *elements* . . .

Martin   Which affected *me* so –

Waxling   They trashed it of course.

Martin   They didn't understand.

Waxling   The intel*lec*tuals.

Martin   They were scared.

Waxling   Join their little club.

Martin   You were ahead of your time.

Waxling   The *guardians*. Of *culture*. Our *heritage*. Our precious *heritage*. You know what heritage is?

Martin   What?

Waxling   It's a Theme Park. With two hundred million personnel managers looking for a salad bar and some fake Elvis in skintights.

Martin   Huh.

Waxling   And me. I'm a voice crying in the Rodeway Inn.

Martin   Dr Waxling. I am here to help you change all that. If you would only let me. (*Pause.*)

Waxling   How much are we talking about?

Martin   How much . . .

Waxling   Money.

Martin   Well . . . the potential, once we get –

Waxling   No, no. How much will you pay me?

Martin   Ah . . . well . . . I wasn't really prepared to get into numbers right –

Waxling   But just for instance.

Martin   How much would you need?

Waxling   I would need at this moment to live and work in the area of five hundred thousand dollars.

Martin   Uh-huh . . .

Waxling   Half a million the book is yours. You own it you do what you want. (*Pause.*)

Martin   That could be arranged.

Waxling   How soon.

Martin   Ah, certainly I could advance you a few thousand up front, then when I –

Waxling   A few thousand.

Martin   Yes, of course once it was all in place you'd be seeing –

Waxling   Where is it now?

Martin   Dr Waxling . . . ah . . . the kind of money you're –

Waxling What do you have now? Right now? Quarter of a million? Let's talk. Hundred thousand? Convince me. How much, come on. (*Pause.*)

Martin I have ... access to financing.

Waxling You have ... *access.*

Martin Yes, there are certain interested parties –

Waxling Give me your wallet.

Martin Huh?

Waxling I want your wallet.

Martin I –

Waxling Wallet. (*Pause.* **Martin** *manages to get out wallet with cuffed hands and offers it to* **Waxling**. **Waxling** *looks through it, finding only two or three bills inside.*)

Martin Dr Waxling ... if you tell me what you're looking for, I would ... I'd be happy to ... um ... (**Waxling** *looks at* **Martin**. *Pause.*) What? (**Waxling** *keeps staring at him.*) What is it?

Waxling This is over.

Martin Dr Waxling, I am *committed* to –

Waxling No, it's all right, really. My fault. I almost took you seriously. You're a nice little tadpole, you shagged my receptionist that's okay.

Martin If you give me some time to, to *structure* –

Waxling Oh please. Go *away*. I'm too old for this. There's nothing to talk about.

Martin Please, Dr Waxling, I *beg* you –

Waxling YOU HAVE NOTHING IN YOUR POCKET. You're no kind of threat here. You're no threat at all. Get yourself some money, young man. Go ... get ... *money*. (*He throws the wallet at* **Martin**.)

Scene Eight

A bus. Day. **Martin**, *asleep. Paperback on seat next to him.* **Bus Driver**, *with plastic trash sack, shaking him.*

Driver   Up and at 'em, Johnny. Let's go.

Martin   Huh?

Driver   All out. Come on. Thank you for choosing Trailways. (*Pause.*)

Martin   What time is it?

Driver   Six a.m.

Martin   Are we in Miami?

Driver   Huh?

Martin   This is Miami?

Driver   This is Provo.

Martin   Can you tell me when we reach Miami?

Driver   Lemme see your ticket. (*Pause.*) You were supposed to change at KC.

Martin   What?

Driver   Miami you had to change at KC. (*Pause.*)

Martin   I'm where?

Driver   Provo. Utah. (**Martin** *puts his face in his hands and starts rocking back and forth.*) Johnny. Hey Johnny. You okay there. Johnny.

Martin   Sorry.

Driver   You sick or something?

Martin   No.

Driver   Somebody you can call?

Martin   I don't think so. (*He stands. Pause.*) Is it cold in Provo?

Driver   Gets cold, yeah. It's cold now.

Martin   You're from Utah?

Driver   Seattle.

Martin   I'm from Florida.

Driver   How about that.

Martin   I grew up in New Jersey.

Driver   It's a big country.

Martin   Yes. (*Pause.*)

Driver (*picking up paperback*)   This yours? (**Martin** *doesn't answer.* **Driver** *drops book in sack.*) Good coffee over the 76 there.

Martin   Thank you. Thank you very much.

Driver   So you gotta get off the bus, okay.

Martin   I will. Certainly. (*Pause.* **Driver** *walks off.*) What am I doing here. What the fuck am I doing here. What the fuck am I doing.

Scene Nine

An office. **Martin** *wolfing down sandwich.* **Kim** *watching him.*

Kim   Some more?

Martin   No, I'm, thank you.

Kim   You're sure.

Martin   *Uh*-huh.

Kim   All right. (*Pause.*) So, Martin.

Martin   Yes.

Kim   You're not looking your best.

Martin   I've been on the road.

Kim   You called me from where?

Martin   The Utah region.

Kim   How is it there?

Martin   I don't know, Kim. I . . . Cold. It was cold.

Kim   Well, you're in New York now.

Martin   Yes.

Kim   How long you here for?

Martin   I don't know.

Kim   Where are you staying?

Martin   I don't know.

Kim   How is business?

Martin   I don't know. I don't have a business. I don't have anything. (*Pause.*)

Kim   What was it you wanted to see me for, Martin?

Martin   Huh?

Kim   When you phoned you said you had to see me.

Martin   Yes. (*Pause.*) Do you recall our conversation last month?

Kim   On the terrace?

Martin   That's right.

Kim   I do indeed.

Martin   I felt we made some sort of connection there. That we believed in the same things. That we knew what was important.

Kim   I'm sure that's absolutely true.

Martin   I've experienced some . . . setbacks since we last met. My plan failed. I failed. I won't bore you with the details. I met Dr Waxling. We discussed my proposal at great length and he was very impressed with . . . (*Pause.*) He couldn't see me as a threat. I didn't present myself as a serious threat and so I failed.

Kim   I regret hearing this.

Martin   No. No. It was the best thing that could have happened. Because I'm clean. Now I *know*. It doesn't matter who I am. It doesn't matter what I believe. There's one thing I need. I need to become a threat. I need to become the biggest threat there is. And that's what I'm going to do. (*Pause.*)

Kim   What was it you wanted to see me for?

Martin   I need half a million dollars now. Later I'll need much more.

Kim   Uh-huh.

Martin   I don't care how I get it.

Kim   Right.

Martin   Do you understand what I'm saying?

Kim   No. I guess I don't. (*Pause.*)

Martin   Kim. You have a *nice* office.

Kim   Thank you.

Martin   You make a lot of money, don't you.

Kim   I'm comfortable.

Martin   Do you need any help in, in what you do?

Kim   I usually work best alone.

Martin   But if someone presented himself to you who was prepared to take risks, would you find a person like that useful? (*Pause.*)

Kim   You don't know what I do.

Martin   I don't care. I mean I do know and it doesn't matter. Whether it's whatever you call it right or wrong, I can't worry about that any more.

Kim   So this thing that I do, you're saying that you'd like to help me do it, despite its dangers and its possible moral or legal complications?

Martin   Yes.

Kim   What is it you think I do? (*Pause.*)

Martin   At the party –

Kim   Which party.

Martin   On the *terrace*, they asked you to leave 'cause . . .

Kim   Because why?

Martin   Because you . . . you're a dealer. Right? A drug dealer. (*Pause.*) Aren't you? (*Pause.*) Kim? (*Pause.*)

Kim   I undertake freelance market analysis for a consortium of Pacific Rim industrial groups.

Martin   What?

Kim   Robot systems. Medical equipment. Information retrieval.

Martin   No.

Kim   Yes.

Martin   No. Oh Jesus. Oh no. God damn it God fucking damn it. What a fuck up I am. What a fuck up loving asshole. What a shit-eating fuckhead. Look at me. Look at me. (**Kim** *looks at him. Pause.*) Kim. I beg your pardon. I've made some very bad assumptions about . . . practically everything. And I . . . Good seeing you. Take care. (*He starts out.*)

Kim   Martin.

Martin   Yes.

Kim   I'd like to offer some advice, if I may.

Martin   What?

Kim   There is nothing so valuable in life as a sense of perspective. (*Pause.*) I am not what you imagined me to be.

Martin   I realize that.

Kim   However, I do know members of my peer group who are. I could arrange for you to meet them. Would you like that?

Martin   Yes.

Kim   All right. (*Pause.*) There are many ways of finding money, Martin. Whatever the climate. Whatever the mood.

Martin   This is what has to be done.

Kim   Well, you're a big boy. (*Pause.*) You don't smoke.

Martin   No.

Kim   I need the nicotine. (*He takes out a cigarette pack and unwraps it.*) It's a curious time, isn't it. I find it curious. Curious to be alive. And change . . . change is *hard.* Honesty, *very* hard. Leaving your desk . . . that's hard. We're not free, you know. All of this and we're still not free. (*Pause.*) You have faith, don't you.

Martin   What?

Kim   Faith. (*Pause.*)

Martin   Yes.

Kim   I envy that. (*He lights a cigarette and takes a long drag.*) Yes yes yes. I'm sensing *all* sorts of possibilities.

Act Two

Scene One

A booth in a restaurant. **Martin** *in new suit,* **Kim**, **Ron**.

Ron   Miami. Miami. Fucking Miami. Fucking skeeve
town. Fucking Cubans. Crazed fucking mothers. I hate
fucking Miami. You're not safe in Miami. How the fuck
you live there I don't know.

Kim   Martin doesn't live in Miami, Ron.

Ron   He doesn't.

Martin   No.

Ron   Where the fuck *does* he live.

Martin   Boca Raton.

Ron   Huh. Well. *You* go down there, huh? Kim? You go
down Miami, right?

Kim   I sometimes go to Miami.

Ron   You're fucking *crazy*. *New* York. *New* York. *New* York.
Last night?

Kim   How was it?

Ron   The best, the best. Absofuckingwhatley the best. Last
night. Okay. We get there. This is at Shea. We get there.
In the limo. I got, I'm with, the, *Carol*, she does the, the,
fuck, you know, that *ad*, the fitness, amazing bod, amazing
bod, fucking amazing bod, and I have, for this occasion, I
put aside my very best, lovely lovely product, for Carol,
who, no, I care about very deeply. So, okay, get to Shea,
it's fucking *bat* night, everybody with the bats, fifty thousand
bat-wielding sociopaths, security is very tight. *I* have a
private booth. In the circle. This is through GE, my little
addictive exec at GE. So we entree, me and Carol, and my
client, I see, has fucked me over, 'cause there's already

someone there, you know who, that talk show guy, he's always got like three drag queens and a Satanist, and he's there with a girl can't be more than fourteen. 'Oops.' This fucking guy, my *daughter* watches that show. And between us, heavy substance abuser. I ask him to leave. I mean I come to watch a ball game with my good friend Carol and I'm forced to encounter skeevy baby-fucking cokeheads. One thing leads to the other, politeness out the window he comes at me Mets ashtray in his hand. What do I do.

Kim   You have a bat.

Ron   I have a bat, I take this bat, I acquaint this individual in the head with this bat. 'Ba-doing.' Right, badoing? He doesn't go down. Stands there, walks out the door, comes back two security guards. 'Is there a problem here, boys?' 'Well sir, this man, bicka bicka bicka,' 'Yes, I completely understand and here's something for your troubles.'

Kim   How much?

Ron   How much, Kim? How much did I give these good men to resolve our altercation? I gave them one thousand dollars in US currency. And they were very grateful. Mr Microphone sits down, doesn't speak, doesn't move rest of the night. Moody fucking person. Mets take it, great ball, home with Carol where we romp in the flower of our youth. I win. I dominate. I get all the marbles. And that is why I love New York.

Kim   Yours is a rich and happy life, Ron.

Ron   Yeah, it is, it is so fuck you, you bogus Ivy League skank. You spent four years sucking bongwater at Hofstra just like me. That's a nice suit.

Kim   You like it?

Ron   How much you pay for it.

Kim   I paid nothing for this suit, Ron. It was a gift.

Ron   Fuck you.

Kim From an admirer.

Ron Fuck *you*. This fucking guy. You know how many times a week he gets laid?

Martin No.

Ron Neither do I. Fifteen years since college I know him, butter wouldn't melt. I don't think it's happened. You ever been laid, Kim?

Kim No, Ron. Never. What's it like.

Ron Fuck you. You get your horn piped by air hostesses every night. You Protestant bastard. That's a nice suit. I don't look good in clothes. (*Pause.*) It's hot. Gonna be a hot summer. (*Pause.*) What are we here for, so?

Kim Martin?

Martin I have a proposition for you, Ron.

Ron This is fine. This is wonderful.

Martin First let me say that I'm a person who's comfortable with risk.

Ron Hmm-*hmm*.

Martin And what I want, what I'd like to *present*, to you, is something we might both find very, um, um . . .

Kim Martin's a businessman, Ron. He understands business. He understands the principles of trust and discretion, and he needs to create some wealth. (**Ron** *looks at* **Martin**. *Pause.*)

Martin Yes. (*Pause.*)

Ron Well. This is very nice. This is most lovely for him and I wish him luck. How does he intend to do these things?

Kim He's going to sell Amway products, Ron. He's going to claw his way to the top of the Amway ladder.

Ron Then fuck *you* with your attitude. I gotta pick up my kid from Dalton twenty minutes, what kind of arrangement you looking for here?

Kim   How are you for blow.

Ron   Ooo, 'blow', listen to him, we bad, we cool, I don't know what you're talking about, I sell landscaping equipment.

Kim   Really.

Ron   You know it.

Kim   Well, Martin's interested in putting in a pond.

Ron   Hmm, how big a pond?

Kim   How big a pond, Martin?

Martin   I . . . (*Pause.*) I've secured an equity loan of two hundred fifty thousand against my property in Florida. (*Pause.*)

Ron   How much?

Martin   Two hundred fi –

Ron (*to* **Kim**)   I don't find you funny any more.

Kim   Oh dear.

Ron   Fuck you think I am, some TV show?

Kim   No, Ron. You're almost too real.

Ron   You fucking bastard.

Martin   What's wrong?

Kim   He's considering your offer.

Ron   No fucking way.

Kim   Being a little short-*sighted*.

Ron   No. No. I'm being smart. We're not hello the Palladium six lines in the toilet any more. The current event, one key a month close personal friends I am a happy man. Quarter million, that is, that is, that puts you in a room very close to a bunch of crazed implacable Colombians with enough firepower send you to Venus in pieces.

Kim   Gee, Dad.

Ron   Hey, these are *serious people*, Kim. They take one look at no offence Mister Rogers here lunch-box full of cash who is he where's he come from the fuck he's *doing* there anyway he wins a prime chance to lose his nut and sit inside a barrel with his dick shoved up his mouth.

Kim   What a dark view of the world, Ron.

Ron   You are such a fucking *tourist*.

Kim   That's me.

Ron   It is you, it is *you*. I got your history Kim, you messed with all kindsa wack shit, you took lotsa pictures, but you never rolled the windows down and that has made you one fucked-up little unit.

Kim   This is really not interesting.

Ron   'Cause you never played your *chances*, buddy, you got plenty a toys but you never played your chances.

Kim   I'm playing them now.

Ron   Too fucking late, you wanna crash and burn go ahead, *I* operate from a position of safety. I don't know why I let myself be seen with you.

Kim   Because I go out of my way introducing responsible people like this man here –

Ron   This man, this man, I don't *know* this man.

Kim   I do. And believe me, let him go you'll regret it.

Ron   'Oh.'

Kim   Yes. *Yes*. Because someone *else* –

Martin   Hold on.

Kim   Someone with vision –

Martin   Kim, let me –

Kim   Is going to, just a sec, profit immensely while you're still peddling your little Glad Bags –

Martin   Kim. *Kim.* Excuse me. I want to *say* something. All right? (*Pause.*)

Kim   Please.

Martin   Thank you. (*Pause.*) Ron. I'd like to see if I can make you understand my, my purpose in coming here, my goals, what I hope to achieve, and the reasons I feel . . . (*Pause.*) No. No. That's pointless. I want you to listen to me. Because this is how it is. All right. There's something I need to get done. I don't have time to waste on . . . *individuals* who won't seize an opportunity. I don't resent them. I don't condemn them. But I will not give them my time. (*Pause.*)

Ron   So?

Martin   So here's what you need to know about me. I have a quarter of a million dollars in cash sitting in a briefcase. I'm eager to spend it. Kim has spoken highly of you. You're aware of my proposal. Either on the boat or off, I have to hear now.

Ron   (*to* **Kim**)   Trying to *threaten* me?

Martin   On or off.

Ron   'Off.' Fuck you. Off.

Martin   Fine. Kim, call me? We'll make new arrangements.

Kim   Mmm-hmm. (**Martin** *gets up and starts out.* **Ron** *looks at* **Kim**.) There you are.

Ron   Wait. Wait. Hey. Hey, um, what's his –

Kim   Martin.

Ron   Martin. Yo. Martin. Come on. Sit down. Everybody with the attitude. Come on now. All right. (*Pause.* **Martin** *returns to the table and sits.*)

Martin Yes?

Ron Wanna be a rich man, huh. (**Martin** *shakes his head.*) Doing this for science?

Martin I'm financing a film.

Ron A film.

Martin A *movie.*

Ron Yeah. Well, um, that makes sense.

Martin I believe it does.

Ron No, I mean, hey, who doesn't go for a little entertainment, right buddy?

Kim Ron, you've captured the matter in its essence. (*Pause.*)

Ron I got stuff, I gotta pick up my daughter, I got dry cleaning.

Kim Righty-o.

Ron This, the thing.

Martin Yes.

Ron I don't know. I'm telling you. I don't know.

Martin What's that mean.

Ron I don't *know*. I'll see what I can *arrange*.

Martin I'm not interested in waiting.

Ron You're not . . . *interested.*

Martin No.

Ron Then fu –

Kim Ron.

Ron What.

Kim I consider us friends.

Ron   So?

Kim   Do something big with your life. For once. (*Pause.*)

Ron   What's it about.

Martin   Huh?

Ron   Your movie.

Martin   It's based . . . (*Pause.*) This creature goes around cracking people's heads open scooping their brains out.

Ron   Well. Whatever. I mean I wouldn't take my kid to see it, you know, what *you* laughing about?

Kim   Nothing, Ron.

Ron   Hey, rot in hell, you heartless fuck. I'm serious. Try a little compassion, huh, it gets you through the day. (*Getting up.*) Drinks on you. (*He exits. Pause.*)

Kim   Hungry at all?

Martin   Goddamn it.

Kim   What's the problem.

Martin   Why did I do that. Why did I *do* that. I *threw* it away.

Kim   Ah no no no.

Martin   I am just so *tired* of little *shits* wasting my time when they can't see past their *own* fear and –

Kim   Martin. You closed this deal. You did. I am very impressed.

Martin   Come on.

Kim   Yes. Listen to me. That was perfect with Ron.

Martin   Why.

Kim   Because I know him. He's weak and he loves money. (*Pause.*) Lesson here for you, though.

Martin   What.

Kim   Have a little more faith in your own abilities. (*Pause.*)

Martin   I will. (**Kim** *looks at menu.*) Kim.

Kim   Hmm.

Martin   What . . . we haven't, what do you want. From this.

Kim   What do you think I should get?

Martin   Te – twenty. Twenty per cent. (*Pause.*) Have I said something wrong?

Kim   No. It's an impressive . . . number.

Martin   You deserve it.

Kim   Let me propose something else.

Martin   What.

Kim   Partnership. (*Pause.*)

Martin   Kim . . . I . . .

Kim   Want to do it for yourself.

Martin   I thought you knew that.

Kim   Yes. (*Pause.*) Most people – I don't mean to be harsh – they have no sense of themselves. They think other people's thoughts. And they waste their lives. That's not for us, Martin. We're better than that and we know it. Now look what we've achieved. Right here at this table, together. I think it's only a start.

Martin   Kim. I'm here to get the movie done.

Kim   What happens after that.

Martin   I can't think about it now.

Kim   I wish you would. I really wish you would. Because you can make a hundred movies, yes, is that all you came for? You can run a studio, own half of midtown net four hundred million per, it's only a bigger desk. I've been there Martin believe me please it's *nothing*, nothing at all. But to do what matters, I mean really *do* something out there in the *world* that frees us from this . . . *junk* . . . that's a life. It's the life I read about. It's the life I want. Don't you? (*Pause.*)

Martin   Staying focused . . .

Kim   Yes.

Martin   On what's important.

Kim   It's not easy.

Martin   No.

Kim   I'll keep you honest. (*Pause.*)

Martin   All right. I . . . Yes. All right.

Kim   (*lifting his drink*)   Well come on then. Let's have an adventure here. (*They toast.*)

Scene Two

A motel room. **Martin** *with briefcase,* **Kim**, **Ron** *with kitchen scales,* **Nuñez**. *Silence.*

Ron   What is that out there?

Kim   Van Wyck Expressway.

Ron   It's like a major fucking highway, huh? Who knew.

Kim   Get out of Manhattan much, Ron?

Ron   Hey, you know how many times I been here Ozone Park? Martin?

Martin   How many times.

Ron   Never. I *never* been to Ozone Park. Looks like fucking *every*place. I never been in a motel room totally skanked as this. Where'd that guy go? It's fifteen fucking minutes.

Kim   Why don't you ask this gentleman?

Ron   'Cause I don't speak *Spanish*. (**Nuñez** *looks at him.*)

Hi. (*Pause.*)

Kim   'A boy sat on a bed, wondering who he might turn out to be.'

Martin   What?

Kim   You know that.

Martin   No.

Kim   First line of the book.

Martin   It is?

Kim   Look it up.

Martin   When this is done I will. (*Pause.*) Thank you.

Ron   Fuck. Ing. Christ. (**Pamfilo** *enters.*)

Pamfilo   Okay. The other car is here.

Ron   Terrific.

Pamfilo   They were caught in the traffic from the stadium.

Ron   Met game, huh, big Met game today, yeah, uh, you like baseball? (*Pause.*)

Pamfilo   Who is Ron again?

Ron   That's me.

Pamfilo   Okay, I am Pamfilo.

Ron   Yeah, right, I know your cousin, we've done business together, I understood he spoke to you, and, ah, how's he doing?

Pamfilo   Eh?

Ron   How's your cousin?

Pamfilo   He's good. (*Pause.*)

Ron   Okay. Well. Ah. This, these are my clients, Mr Feston, Mr Mirkheim.

Pamfilo   Yes.

Ron   Your cousin met them. Very reliable, dependable gentlemen.

Martin   How do you do. (*Pause.*)

Ron   So. (*Pause.*)

Pamfilo   Los registraste?

Nuñez   No son nada.

Pamfilo   Que te dijo, siempre tienes cuidad con todos. (*To the others.*) Nuñez, he is my . . . security man, okay? He is going to see that everything is safe between us. (**Nuñez** *frisks* **Ron**, **Kim** *and* **Martin**.)

Ron   Very sensible.

Pamfilo   Yes. Because sometimes men are not honourable.

Kim   Isn't that unfortunate.

Pamfilo   For them it is.

Ron   Ha. Right right right.

Pamfilo   Who is with the money?

Martin   Me.

Pamfilo   Yes. May I look please. (**Martin** *hands him the briefcase.* **Pamfilo** *opens it but does not look inside.*) We have met before.

Martin   Pardon?

Pamfilo   You and I.

Martin   I don't think so.

Pamfilo   No? Someone who is like you.

Martin   Well.

Pamfilo   That's right. The man I am thinking of, he is a good man. He provides for his family and respects the memory of his mother.

Martin   Does he.

Pamfilo   Yes. Are you a good man, my friend?

Martin   I hope so.

Pamfilo   You're not sure, huh?

Martin   I am.

Pamfilo   Then I know you would never try and cheat me.

Martin   No. (*Pause.* **Pamfilo** *closes the briefcase.*)

Pamfilo (*to* **Nuñez**)   Ve al auto y traeme la bolsa. (*To* **Martin**.) He is going to bring it.

Martin   Great. (**Nuñez** *exits. Silence.*)

Ron   So, what, you live in the city there, Pamfilo? (*Pause.*)

Pamfilo   No. (*Pause.*) Hempstead.

Ron   Out on the Island, huh. That's terrific. Lot a, lot a, lot a Colombians, Hempstead?

Pamfilo   I'm from Honduras.

Ron   Say what?

Pamfilo   Honduras. It's a country. It's in America. (*Pause. Silence.*)

Martin   How . . .

Pamfilo   Yes.

Martin   How long have you been in, in our land.

Pamfilo   Three years. Since I'm nineteen.

Martin   How do you like it. (*Pause.*)

Pamfilo   You work hard . . . use your head . . . you can be very big. (**Kim** *laughs.*) That's funny, huh?

Ron (*under his breath*)   Shut *up*, Kim.

Pamfilo   Hey, you think I'm funny?

Martin   Why don't we –

Pamfilo   I'm not so good as you, is that it? Hey.

Kim   No. I'm just enchanted by your optimism. And I sincerely hope that all your dreams come true. (*Pause.*)

Pamfilo   Thank you. (**Nuñez** *enters with suitcase.*) Here is what you want. (**Nuñez** *hands the suitcase to him. He opens it and displays contents.*) Okay?

Martin   Maybe.

Pamfilo   Try some. (*He takes out a Saran-wrapped package of coke, opens it, and offers it to* **Martin**. **Kim** *steps up, reaches into the suitcase and takes out a different package, opens it and samples it.*)

Kim   This has possibilities.

Pamfilo   It's what you're looking for, huh.

Martin   Means to an end.

Pamfilo   What's that.

Martin   This will . . . *get* us . . . where we have to go.

Pamfilo   Yes. I understand.

Kim   I'd like to weigh it.

Pamfilo   It's twelve kilos, what we said.

Kim   I'm sure it is, but . . .

Pamfilo   You don't trust me?

Kim   We just want to weigh it. (*To* **Ron**.) Isn't that what they do on TV?

Pamfilo   What. You think I am trying to cheat you?

Ron   Hey, *no* one's saying that.

Pamfilo   He's saying it.

Ron   Just, we're, a precaution –

Pamfilo (*to* **Martin**)   I take you on your honour, my friend, this is how you treat me?

Ron   Shit . . .

Martin   I'm not doubting –

Pamfilo   This is no good. No. No this is bad business. We don't do it. Here's the money. This is bad, very bad. Nuñez. (**Nuñez** *starts out.* **Pamfilo** *follows.*)

Martin   Wait. Wait. What do we do . . .

Ron   Forget about it.

Martin   No. Pamfilo. Come on. Let's – We can make this work. We *can*. Kim? Please. (*Pause.* **Nuñez** *re-enters.* **Pamfilo** *looks at* **Martin**. *He takes the suitcase and opens it.*)

Pamfilo   You take one. Whatever one. Take it and weigh it. They all the same. They all a kilo. I don't think like you. (**Martin** *takes a package from the case. He puts it on the scales.* **Pamfilo** *looks at* **Nuñez**. *Pause.*)

Ron   Two and a quarter, touch under.

Pamfilo   That's a kilo. That's exactly a kilo. Here's another one. Go ahead.

Martin   It's all right.

Pamfilo   Go on.

Kim   Make the boy happy, Martin.

Martin   Kim. That's enough. (*Pause.*) Pamfilo. My apologies. Please. (**Pamfilo** *looks at* **Martin**, *closes suitcase and offers it to him.* **Martin** *takes it. He hands* **Pamfilo** *the money.*)

Pamfilo   Este payaso no sabe ni papa.

Martin   What?

Pamfilo   Always know your friends. (*He exits with* **Nuñez**. **Martin** *takes package off scales, puts it back in case and shuts it.*)

Kim   Well.

Martin   Right.

Kim (*offering his hand*)   We're in it now. (*Pause.*)

Martin (*taking it*)   Yes.

Kim   No. We're *in* it. We're really *in* it. *Everything's* going to happen.

Martin   One less thing in the way. (**Kim** *sees* **Ron** *staring at the floor.*)

Kim   Something on your mind, Ron?

Ron   Yeah. Let's give me my cut and get the fuck out of here as rapidly as possible.

Scene Three

A rec room. **Martin**, **Kim** *with briefcase. Late.*

Martin   How do you know this guy?

Kim   Shared a house one summer. He was doing three grams a day. (*Pause.*)

Martin   I grew up around here.

Kim   Did you.

Martin   My parents bought a place. Paid cash. Big moment for them. Saved up, fourteen years. 1968.

Kim   Ancient times.

Martin   Yeah. (*Pause.*) This afternoon, Kim. The motel.

Kim   Mmm-hmm.

Martin   Don't act that way again. Okay.

Kim   Why not.

Martin   I don't like it. (*Pause.*) We have to agree what we're doing stays normal. I am calling it business and that's how I need it to be.

Kim   You're just tired.

Martin   It's how I need it, Kim.

Kim   I have a business, Martin. It's in an office. I'm there every day. We discussed something else.

Martin   That was talking. This has to get *done* I cannot afford any risks. Do we understand each other? (*Pause.*) Kim. Do we –

Lee (*entering*)   Sorry. Had to switch the security system back on. Press the wrong button I get the Short Hills police force storming the pool deck.

Kim   Can't be too safe.

Lee   You can't, you can't. Kim, get you a drink? Marvin?

Martin   Martin. No thank you, Lee.

Lee   Fair enough. Serious man. Welcome to New Jersey. You guys have trouble getting here?

Kim   No.

Lee   Hit traffic?

Martin   Not this time of night.

Lee   Yeah. Look. I apologize for that. My schedule's been, you don't wanna know, I'm not even getting home 'til eleven. I don't see my wife, the twins, forget it.

Kim   Working you hard, huh, Lee.

Lee   Sucking me dry, Kim. But it's worth it. We got the jump on the primaries. 'Cause the momentum is there. Uh. Uh. Organization is there. Money's there. We're diving straight into the Grown-Up Pool. Really. I mean this one counts, and, uh, uh . . . (*Pause.*) Yeah, I'm sorry, what was I saying?

Martin   Something that counts.

Lee   Right, exactly.

Kim   Lee's consulting for Paul Kinsen.

Martin Who?

Lee Senator Kinsen. Arizona.

Martin You consult on . . . ?

Lee Chief of Media Relations actually. Got the whole campaign.

Kim Congratulations.

Lee And all I had to do was blow him.

Martin Excuse me?

Lee I'm kidding of course. Great opportunity for me, something *big*.

Kim Old Mr Stars and Jackboots.

Lee What are you, some pansy Democrat?

Kim I'm a registered bystander.

Lee Look at Kinsen this year. Try Kinsen out. Kinsen could be very very good for you.

Kim Why's that.

Lee 'Cause he wants to win and he's primed to kick ass.

Kim I'm loving it.

Lee Which is what I'm saying. He's the man for the nineties. This guy takes no prisoners. Is that what you want in a Great White Father? I think so. Check this out, what do you think, dummy ad, national spot, wanna hear it, okay, great. (*He picks up a stack of storyboards.*) What it is, should be, is a *movie*, a little thirty-second movie about something we want to say. Desert, morning light, very pure, very 'American'. Uh, uh, uh, young boy, blond hair, big horse. Tries to climb on. Can't. Falls off. Hits hard. Eats dirt. You with me?

Martin Yes.

Lee Voiceover: 'There are some who believe the best is behind us. Some who think we've lost the way. Some who feel that fear rules the length and breadth of a once proud land.' Dramatic Pause. Kid stands up. Tight on the face. V.O: 'Paul Kinsen believes differently. He believes in a nation whose future means more than its past. He believes in a nation unafraid of its strength. He believes in a nation of dreams. Because dreams can be real.' Kid slaps the dust off. Beat. 'If we want them to be.' Kid grabs the stirrup, whatever. He's up. He's on. He's riding. He's a winner. *And* dissolve to Kinsen, presidential as hell. Super titles: 'Paul Kinsen. Believe ... the ... what.' Believe the what, huh. Believe the something. What's good to believe in.

Martin Are you asking me?

Lee I'm stuck at the tag. Breaking my balls Kinsen this fucking presentation. Know what he's saying? 'Why can't it be me on a horse?' I mean I'm on the team ten thousand per cent but Wonder Chimp the man isn't, please, I didn't say that. What do we believe in here, *I* don't know, I don't, I honestly don't, no idea. Boom boom boom.

Martin How about possibilities.

Lee Huh?

Martin Believe the possibilities. We all believe in possibilities, don't we, keeps us going.

Lee 'Believe the Possibilities.'

Martin You got it.

Kim That's amusing, Martin.

Lee 'Paul Kinsen: Believe the Possibilities.' Yum dum dum ba dum bum ba bum bum. Hell does that mean.

Martin What do you think it means.

Lee It means, I don't know, Go for the Gusto, Be All You Can Be, Ram Tough, it means whatever you want it to mean, it doesn't mean anything, it sounds good. Am I right? Is that it? Hello? (*Pause.*)

Martin Yes. That's it exactly.

Lee (*to* **Kim**)   What flew up his ass?

Kim   Past his bedtime.

Martin   I'm fine.

Kim   You'd better be, friend. (*They look at each other.* **Martin** *turns away.*)

Martin   Let's get down to business.

Lee   *Yes.*

Martin   This has to be a cash –

Kim   *Ma*rtin and I have something very special here, Lee. I want you to *know* you're the first person we thought of.

Lee   Thank you. I'm excited.

Kim   You should be.

Lee   Little *surprised* . . .

Kim   Why's that.

Lee   I didn't know you were dealing.

Kim   Disappointed?

Lee   Well, you know. It's a step. It's a grey area.

Kim   I like me in grey.

Lee   Yeah, right. Boom boom boom.

Martin   We discussed possibly a couple of kilos.

Lee   Well, a couple, one, I'm getting off it, but if the quality –

Martin   The quality is superb.

Lee   'Cause what I *been* buying –

Kim   We hear you.

Lee   It doesn't really get me, it just doesn't seem to get me as, it doesn't seem to *give* me the same feeling of . . .

Kim   Uh-huh.

Lee The same, uh, uh, uh . . .

Martin Strength.

Lee Yeah. Strength. Strength. Yeah. Yeah. (*Pause.*) And I won't fuck with crack, you know. I won't. 'Cause that's really, that is a very *bad*, um . . . problem.

Kim Then Lee, absolutely is this for you. (*He takes kilo bag out of the briefcase and lays it before* **Lee**.) Look at that.

Lee Hmm.

Kim Shines just like mica.

Lee Yeah, this could be good for me.

Kim I think so.

Lee 'Cause I *need* it.

Kim Go ahead. (**Lee** *tries some. Pause.*) What did I tell you? (**Lee** *says nothing.*) Now I want you to know that there is plenty more if –

Lee What are you doing here, Kim?

Kim Excuse me?

Lee I don't, is this a joke?

Kim No.

Martin What's the problem?

Lee This is garbage.

Kim No. I've *tried* it, Lee.

Lee You have.

Kim Yes, and it's the best coke you can –

Lee Bullshit.

Kim Lee –

Lee *Bull*shit. This is what you buy outside the Port

Authority before you catch the bus. I'm past this, I'm *way*
past it, you think you're gonna fool me? (*Pause.* **Kim** *tries*
some.)

Martin   What's happening, Kim.

Kim   Hold on a second.

Lee   This won't even get my *tongue* high.

Kim   Give me a *second*, Lee.

Lee   Asking for big money you better –

Kim   Shut up. Lee, okay.

Lee   Hey, this is my *house*, buddy, you don't speak to
me –

Martin   Kim –

Kim   YES, GIVE ME ONE *SECOND* PLEASE THANK
YOU. (*Pause.*) The cases.

Martin   What?

Kim   The motel. They switched cases.

Martin   I don't –

Kim   They *switched cases*. They forced the *argument*, he
stepped into the hall, they came back we weighed the kilo –

Martin   No.

Lee   Hey, you wanna keep it down –

Kim   They took us.

Martin   No. No.

Kim   We *sucked* it up –

Martin   But they, he offered –

Kim   Stupid *white* boys and they *took* us.

Martin   No. No. There's a deal. You – We have a *deal*.

You're gonna buy this.

Lee   Keep dreaming.

Martin   You're buying. God*damn* you. You have to *buy* – (**Terry**, **Lee***'s wife, enters in robe.*)

Lee   Don't threaten me, Pee Wee, I don't buy jack from you, hi honey, are we too loud?

Terry   What's going on . . .

Lee   Hon, ah, you remember Kim Feston from the *summer*.

Terry   . . . Half awake and I, hello . . .

Kim   How are the twins, Terry.

Terry   Oh, they're . . .

Lee   Kim and his friend are very interested in fund raising for Senator Kinsen, we're just connecting on it, they want to help us along see if they can make a difference.

Terry   It's late, Lee. You're never going to get up.

Lee   I know, I'll, in a minute. Really. (*Pause.*)

Terry   Anybody want tea?

Lee   No sweetie, thank you. (*Pause.*)

Terry   Well come to bed soon. (**Lee** *nods. She exits. Pause.*)

Martin   Oh my god. What have I done.

Lee   Excuse me. Over here. This is *my* rec room you're sitting in. I got a wife and two baby kids upstairs, I got a presentation due nine o'clock in the morning, and I have NO FUCKING WAY of getting high tonight. So would you please leave.

Kim   Lee, I suggest –

Lee   You have nothing to say to me, Kim. You just went belly up.

Scene Four

A car. **Martin**, **Kim** *behind wheel. Silence.*

Martin   That was the turn-off.

Kim   What?

Martin   That was the turn-off for New York. (*Pause.*)

Kim   I'll take the next exit.

Martin   Yah.

Kim   We'll turn around.

Martin   'Kay. (*Pause.*) I'm fucked, Kim.

Kim   Stop it.

Martin   I am. I'm *fucked*. I'm *so* fucked.

Kim   That's not *helping*, all right.

Martin   You don't understand the position –

Kim   We had a setback. We were too eager. We made a mistake, that's done. We move on.

Martin   Where. Where do we move *to*.

Kim   We can sell the coke. It's a garbage cut but we can sell it.

Martin   For how much.

Kim   Less.

Martin   To who?

Kim   Somebody stupid.

Martin   Who?

Kim   I have to think about it.

Martin   You don't *know*.

Kim   I have to *think*. I have to work it *out*.

Martin   Do you know what you're doing, Kim? Do you?

I really need to find out. Do you have any *idea?*

Kim   There's always possibilities.

Martin   The *money* –

Kim   You don't care about money.

Martin   But *my* money, Kim. That was *my* – I mean it was a loan. You *know* that. I can't pay that back. I was counting on the, the . . . I don't *have* it. You understand? Anywhere. I'm *already*. . . . Here it is. Okay. I've been bad about money. I'm in a, a, *situation* with it and I don't see how I can get out. It's going to bury me, Kim. I'm really afraid it's going to bury me and – (*Rotating lights of a squad car start flashing behind them.*) Oh fuck.

Kim   It's all right.

Martin   What's happening?

Kim   I don't know.

Martin   Were we speeding?

Kim   We'll find out.

Martin   It's not us, I'm sure it's not, don't stop, what are you doing –

Kim   Hide the briefcase, would you, Martin.

Martin   What?

Kim (*pulling car over*)   Hide the briefcase please. Under the seat.

Martin   This is not me. This is not where I'm supposed to be . . .

Kim   It would be a good idea to hurry up right now.

Martin   It won't *fit*.

Kim   I'm sure it will.

Martin (*trying to jam it under*)   It won't. It won't. Oh fuck what am I doing here.

Kim   Martin. Stop it. Stop it. All right. It's just a briefcase. Everybody has one. (**State Trooper** *approaches with nightstick-style flashlight in hand.*) There is absolutely nothing to get alarmed about. (**Trooper** *comes up to driver's side.*) Officer.

Trooper   Posted speed limit on this parkway is fifty-five miles an hour.

Kim   Yes.

Trooper   You're clocked on radar at seventy-six.

Kim   Yes. Of course.

Trooper   See your licence, please.

Kim   Certainly. (**Trooper** *inspects licence. Pause.*)

Martin   Just got a little lost on our way back to the city.

Trooper   Which city is that.

Martin   New York.

Trooper   I've heard of it.

Martin   Right. Ha.

Kim   Officer, it's late, I understand the violation, please we'll just take the ticket.

Trooper   Rushing off to bed, huh.

Martin   We have a big presentation to make first thing in the morning.

Trooper   Do you.

Martin   Yes.

Trooper   Back there in New York.

Martin   That's correct. (**Trooper** *shines light into car. Briefcase is on* **Martin***'s lap. He looks straight ahead at nothing.*)

Kim   I tell you, next time I set the cruise control and forget about it. (*Pause.*) You know?

Martin What?

Kim (*to* **Trooper**)   Creeps up on you, check the
speedometer and –

Trooper Could you both step out of the car, please?

Martin What for?

Trooper I'm asking you to.

Kim Is this really necessary?

Trooper If you want it to be. (*Pause.*)

Kim Fine. Let me turn the engine off.

Trooper Uh-huh. (**Kim** *shuts off engine and drops the keys.*)

Kim Great. (*Hunching over.*) I dropped my keys. I'm sorry.
Could you just shine your light here. One sec.

Trooper (*leaning in*)   Where.

Kim Right here. (*Coming up.*) Okay. I found them. (*He has
a small calibre pistol in his hand.*)

Martin Kim, are you – (**Kim** *grabs the flashlight and shoots
the* **Trooper** *point-blank in the face. Pause.*)

Kim Look what I've done.

Scene Five

A field by a road. **Martin** *with* **Trooper***'s flashlight,* **Kim**
smoking cigarette.

Kim Where are we?

Martin I don't know.

Kim Sky's lit up in that direction.

Martin It's a refinery. They're all up and down here.
We should have stayed on the Parkway.

Kim You might want to shut that off. (**Martin** *shuts off
flashlight. Pause.*)

Martin   What are we going to do.

Kim   I'm going to enjoy this cigarette.

Martin   Why didn't you tell me Kim.

Kim   You know I've been afraid, I'll say it now, really afraid. Afraid to be *tested*. Afraid I wouldn't be strong. But I *was*. I *was*. You *saw* that I was, God I feel –

Martin   Kim, you should have *told* me.

Kim   What did you want to know, I was *ready*, he stood there and – look how this hand's shaking –

Martin   That you had a *gun*, a fucking *gun*.

Kim   Can't have an adventure without a gun.

Martin   Fuck adventure this was my *business*.

Kim   Whatever you want to call it.

Martin   No Kim, no, my *business* we were conducting, not some, some, in the street that you read about, a guy some bracelet he gets . . . *shot* Jesus *Christ* there's blood on my shirt.

Kim   Would you rather be arrested?

Martin   I don't know.

Kim   You must have an *opinion*.

Martin   I DON'T KNOW. MY BRAIN'S GONE AND I CAN'T *THINK* ANY MORE. (*Pause.*)

Kim   Let me tell you something, Martin. It might help you, because it's true. Everything . . . *everything* up this exact moment . . . is the Past. We're done with it. You're concerned about that policeman? I am not. It's so clear to me. What did he want to do? Take what we have and punish us. By whose authority? Not mine, Martin. Not mine. This is so *clear* now. It's a dead little planet we're standing on. I'm alive. And I don't need to be forgiven one goddamn thing. Do you? (*Pause.*) Now we have several possibilities spread before us. We can go on debating ethics in the middle of a marsh. We can ease up to the next state trooper and turn ourselves in. Or we can drive back to Manhattan secure in the knowledge that we are two polite young white men in well-cut suits and will . . . not . . . be . . . touched. Because we set the standards. And we judge *ourselves* accordingly. (*Pause.*) It's freedom, Martin. I am talking to you about being free. (*Pause.*)

Martin I'm done.

Kim What's that mean.

Martin I'm finished with it.

Kim Just like that.

Martin Yes.

Kim I thought you wanted to be a threat.

Martin I don't know what I 'wanted to *be*'. I can't *remember*. I've eaten myself up and there's nothing left. *Nothing.*

Kim You're very weak. Aren't you.

Martin I *am*, so fuck it. Fuck the coke. Fuck the money, fuck *all* money. And fuck the movie. I won't make it. Who was I kidding. It's shit anyway –

Kim Is it.

Martin *Yes*, let's say it, that book is just *shit.* Some fucking fantasy about power and, and, 'everything is possible', where *are* they, where are these 'possibilities'. I don't see them, *this* is it, this is life and that's ALL IT WILL EVER BE.

Kim Where are you going, Martin.

Martin To find the highway. Let go of me.

Kim That's a bad idea, Martin. (**Martin** *keeps walking.*) Martin. This is your mess.

Martin   Fuck it.

Kim   Your *mess*, Martin, I won't get stuck with it . . .
(**Martin** *keeps walking.*) Hey. You. Little man. (*He takes out
the gun and shoots.* **Martin** *shouts and falls.* **Kim** *starts towards
him.*) I *bet* that hurts, huh.

Martin   You bastard . . . we're *part*ners . . .

Kim   You just changed that didn't you. (*He reaches
Martin.*) Finish what you start. (*He puts the gun against
Martin*'s head.*)

Martin   Kim. Please.

Kim   Hmm.

Martin   I can't face it, I can't, I can't, I'm scared, I'm so
scared . . .

Kim   I'm sorry for you. (*He pulls the trigger. Gun jams. Pause.*)
Would you give me that?

Martin   What?

Kim   Give me the flashlight please?

Martin   No . . .

Kim   Come on.

Martin   HELP ME! SOMEBODY HELP ME!

Kim   Shh. Quiet. Don't be frightened.

Martin   *Fuck* you . . .

Kim   Yes, all right. Just give me the flashlight. Come on.
You know you're not up to this. Give me the flashlight
everything will be okay. Nothing to get alarmed about.
You're safe. You are. You really are. (*Pause.*)

Martin   Here. (*He butts **Kim** in the face with the flashlight.
Kim staggers back.* **Martin** *clubs him again, swinging wildly.*)
You *want* this? You *want* it? Take it, *take* it!

Kim   Martin – okay –

Martin   HERE'S YOUR THREAT.

Kim (*collapsing*)   Uh –

Martin   HERE'S YOUR POSSIBLE. HERE'S YOUR
SAFETY, YOU FEEL THAT? (**Kim** *stops moving.* **Martin**
keeps beating him.) GET UP. GET UP. I'M READY. I AM
NOT AFRAID. I AM. NOT AFRAID. (**Kim** *lies face down.*
Martin *lowers his arms. Long pause.*) Kim. Hey. Look at this.
Look at it you fuck. (*He pushes* **Kim** *over with his foot and
displays the flashlight barrel.*) That's your blood. You see it?
That's *your* blood. Here's what I know. I'm stronger than
you.

Scene Six

Radio Announcer (*V.O. in blackout*)   . . . In local Jersey
news, police are pursuing what they call 'several promising
leads' in last week's brutal slaying of Officer Thomas Selby,
an eight-year veteran of the Highway Patrol. Selby was shot
point-blank in the face when he stopped a motorist just
south of the Irvington exit on the Garden State. He will be
buried with full honours tomorrow. In a separate incident,
investigators are still hoping to identify the body of a man
found bludgeoned to death near the Linden refinery fields
Wednesday morning. The man was described as white,
well-dressed, approximately thirty-five years old. Police are
considering the possibility that the murder was drug related.
They have no leads at this time.

Scene Seven

A private office. Bright sun. Big desk. **Carling** *standing with
briefcase, waiting.* **Martin** *enters.*

Martin (*extending his hand*)   Mr Carling.

Carling   Mr Powers. (*They shake.*)

Martin   Sorry to keep you hanging. Welcome to
California.

Carling   Thank you.

Martin   Bet you don't get out here much.

Carling   First time.

Martin   Well. Happy New Year. Make way for tomorrow, huh?

Carling   Ready or not. (*Pause. He notices poster.*) That one of yours?

Martin   Oh yes.

Carling   *Dead World.*

Martin   Buckets-of-blood quickie. Did it for half a million and it looks it. Got us started though.

Carling   Huh.

Martin   We're doing a big one now. Big picture. Very proud.

Carling   What is it.

Martin   Based on a book, ah, wonderful wonderful story, about a little guy overcomes all the odds to make his dream a reality. It's upbeat, it's about winners, and, uh . . . it'll be great.

Carling   Sounds exciting.

Martin   Tell you the truth, this point in my life, I'd rather watch my son play softball. You have children, Mr Carling?

Carling   Afraid not.

Martin   It changes you. Truly changes you. (*Pause.*)

Carling   Mr Powers, I think you know we have a problem.

Martin   We seem to, and I thank you for getting in touch with me.

Carling   Certain evidence has come into my possession that links you to Mr Martin Mirkheim, the subject of my investigation.

Martin   What evidence is that.

Carling   It arises out a settlement by Far Horizon Films, I believe that's your company, to a Dr Waxling for non-payment and breach of contract.

Martin   Mirkheim.

Carling   That's right.

Martin   Don't know who you're talking about. (*Pause.*)

Carling   Mr Powers. Tax evasion is a serious crime and the State of Florida will vigorously pursue prosecution.

Martin   As well they should.

Carling   I hoped my visit here would give you an opportunity to come to terms with the situation.

Martin   You mentioned that on the phone. I'm not sure what your point is.

Carling   My point . . . is that back taxes are the least of Mr Mirkheim's concerns. (*He opens his briefcase and removes a manila folder.*) Would you like to see my hobby? (*As he sorts through papers inside.*) Notice of seizure, collateral on defaulted equity loan, this is years ago . . . old credit card statements, also unpaid. . . . Divorce granted in absentia, Palm Beach County Court . . . just bits and pieces, nobody bothers with them . . .

Martin   Mr Carling, I have a busy –

Carling   Sworn deposition, motorist Garden State Parkway, night of April 23, 1991 . . . not my field but I happen to be curious . . . (*He picks up a Polaroid photo from folder.*) A New York City businessman. (*He places it on the desk.*) He's dead now. (**Martin** *doesn't look.*) No interest in history, Mr Powers?

Martin   I prefer the future. It's more hopeful.

Carling   Well, at this moment, your future is what you make of it, I'd say.

Martin   Would you. (*Pause.*) You know the worst thing a man can do, Mr Carling? He can undertake an adventure. He can misjudge his strength. And he can destroy himself. (*He reaches into his desk and brings out a thick envelope and a gun.*) One of these is for you. (*Offering envelope.*) Is it this? (*As* **Carling** *hesitates.*) Check inside to be sure. Go ahead. (**Carling** *takes envelope and looks inside.*)

Carling   This *is* mine. Thank you.

Martin   Don't mention it. (*Of file.*) That stays.

Carling   Of course. (*He places the folder on the desk.*)

Martin   Is there something else to discuss?

Carling   I don't think so.

Martin   Then you keep *safe* in California. Okay?

Carling   Yes. (*He exits.* **Martin** *watches him go. Pause.*)

Martin   (*into intercom*)   Nothing 'til I buzz. (*He places the gun back in the desk, then reaches for the folder. He looks through the contents, turning the pages slowly. To himself.*) Focus. Stay *focused* . . . (*He reaches for the lighter on his desk.*) Keep ready. (*He sets the folder aflame, holding it in his hand.*) Be strong. (*He drops it in the wastebasket as it continues to burn.* **Martin** *sits at his desk, looking straight out. Lights fade.*)

Boys' Life
&
Search and Destroy

'*Boys' Life* is the most balanced and intelligent comment on the battle of the sexes I've seen in a long time.'
New Yorker

'*Search and Destroy* is brimful of dramatic energy and pitch-black humour, and comes over like a rancid reworking for the 1990s of Arthur Miller's *Death of a Salesman*.'
Daily Telegraph

Howard Korder was born in New York City and received a BA in Theatre from the State University of New York in Binghamton. His first play, *Night Maneuver*, was produced in 1982 by the Floating Rep. *Episode 26* was presented Off-Broadway by the Lamb's Theater in 1985. The Manhattan Punchline produced *Lip Service* the following year. *Fun* premiered at the Actor's Theater of Louisville's 1987 Human Festival (Heidmann Award for Best One-Act Play). Its companion piece, *Nobody*, was selected for the 1987 O'Neill Playwrights Conference (winner, HBO Writer's Award). Both plays were subsequently presented in New York at the Manhattan Punchline, the American Repertory Theater in Cambridge and numerous other theatres in the US and Canada. In 1988, *Boys' Life* premiered at the Mitzi E. Newhouse Theater at the Lincoln Center (nominated for the Pulitzer Prize) and HBO broadcast Korder's television adaptation of *Lip Service* (Cable Ace Award for Best Comedy Special). *Search and Destroy* was commissioned and premiered by California's South Coast Repertory in 1990 (Los Angeles Theater Critics' Award for Best New Play and Joseph Kesselring Prize from the National Art Club). It was subsequently produced at Yale Rep, on Broadway and at the Royal Court, directed by Stephen Daldry. A film version, produced by Martin Scorcese, was released in 1995. *The Lights* premiered at New York's Lincoln Center in 1993 (winner, Obie Award) and performed at the Royal Court in 1996. A commissioned one-act play, *Ted Williams*, was produced in June 1995 at the Magic Theater, San Francisco, as part of an evening entitled *Hitting for the Cycle*. He is the recipient of the 1996 Guggenheim Fellowship in playwriting.

Lightning Source UK Ltd.
Milton Keynes UK
UKOW03f0014290517
302214UK00001B/5/P